The complete book of
Crochet

TREASURE PRESS

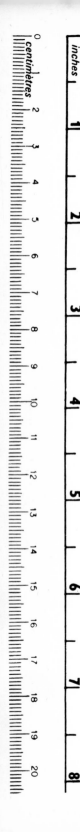

Photographs on pages 27, 33, 37, 41, 45, 53, 57, 61, 63, 73, 77, 81, 85, 93 by Jason Biggs Studios

The publishers wish to thank G-plan galleries for the use of accessories for photography

First published by Octopus Books Limited
This edition published by Treasure Press
59 Grosvenor Street
London W1

© 1973 Octopus Books Limited

Reprinted 1983

ISBN 0 907812 23 6

Printed in Hong Kong

Contents

Crochet for the home

Fashion crochet

Crochet for children

Gifts to make

Comparative needle sizes

Crochet hooks are available in steel for working with fine cotton yarns, and in aluminium or plastic for coarser cottons, wools and synthetic yarns. The size of hook you use depends on the weight and type of yarn you are working with, and crochet patterns usually recommend which size this should be. The important thing however is not necessarily to use the precise hook size quoted but to check your tension first by working a small sample in the stitch pattern. Provided you achieve the correct tension [gauge] as given in the instructions it does not matter

what size hook you use. The sizings of croc[ ]hooks have been standardized. The chart below shows the actual size of hooks in the International Standard sizes in relation to old U.K. and the American sizes. Australian, Canadian and South African si[ ]are the same as old UK sizes.

New Milward international range	Old English range	American range
	8 *(steel)*	
	7	
	6·50	
0·60 *(steel)*	6	
	5·50	
0·75	5	
	4·50	
1	4	
	3·50	
1·25	3	
1·50	2·50	
1·75	2	
	1·50	
2 *(aluminium)*	14 *(aluminium)*	
2·50	12	B/1
	11	C/2
3·50	10	D/3
	9	E/4
4	8	F/5
4·50	7	G/6
5	6	H/8
5·50	5	H/8
6	4	I/9
	3	J/10
7	2	K/10¼

Introduction

Now, when more and more people are discovering the full potential of the craft of crochet, this book provides a complete introduction as well as a variety of designs to make. The word crochet is derived from the French 'crochet' meaning hook. Traditionally consisting of lacy patterns, crochet was once used mainly to make decorative mats and edgings. Recently, however, modern designs and colours have widened the scope of the craft.

Crochet is basically simple, despite the intricate appearance of the work. This book contains easy-to-follow, illustrated instructions and diagrams for the stitches. These show both the right-handed and the left-handed person how to do the basic chain stitch and its variations. Once these are mastered, the craft is immensely satisfying as the work grows so quickly.

The designs in this book include both traditional and modern patterns. According to the yarn and the stitch used, there are cobwebby lace patterns and bolder modern designs. There are articles to make for the home and as gifts, as well as fashion designs and things to make for children.

Abbreviations

	English	American
ch	*chain*	*chain*
dc	*double crochet*	*single crochet*
hlf tr	*half treble*	*half double crochet*
tr	*treble*	*double crochet*
dbl tr	*double treble*	*treble crochet*
trip tr	*triple treble*	*double treble*
quad tr	*quadruple treble*	*triple treble*
quin tr	*quintuple treble*	*quadruple treble*
sp(s)	*space(s)*	
st(s)	*stitch(es)*	
ss	*slip stitch*	
sp(s)	*space(s)= 2 ch, miss 2 ch or tr, 1 tr into next ch or tr,*	
blk(s)	*block(s)= 4 tr plus 3 tr for each additional block in group.*	

* Asterisk *Repeat instructions following the asterisks as many more times as specified in addition to the original.*

For example * 1 dc into next cluster, 1 dc into next loop, 2 ch, 1 tr into next dc, 2 ch, 1 dc into next loop; repeat from * 9 times more, means that there are 10 patterns in all.

( ) *Repeat instructions in brackets as many times as specified.*

For example, '(3 ch, 1 dc into next sp) 5 times', means to make all that is in parenthesis 5 times in all.

Tension (gauge)

Check this carefully before commencing your design as only the correct tension (gauge) will ensure the best finished specimens. If your crochet is loose use a size finer hook, if tight use a size larger hook.

Laundering crochet

Use a warm lather of pure soap flakes and wash in the usual way, either by hand or washing machine. If desired, the article may be spin-dried until it is damp, or left until it is half dry. Place a piece of paper, either plain white or squared, on top of a clean, flat board. Following the correct measurements, draw the shape of the finished article on to the paper, using ruler and set square for squares and rectangles and a pair of compasses for circles. Using rustless pins, pin the crochet out to the pencilled shape, taking care not to strain the crochet. Pin out the general shape first, then finish by pinning each picot, loop or space into position. Special points to note carefully when pinning out are:

(a) When pinning loops, make sure the pin is in the centre of each loop to form balanced lines.

(b) When pinning scallops, make all the scallops the same size and regularly curved.

(c) Pull out all picots.

(d) Where there are flowers, pull out each petal in position.

(e) When pinning filet crochet, make sure that the spaces and blocks are square and that all edges are even and straight. If the crochet requires to be slightly stiffened, use a solution of starch (1 dessertspoonful to 1 pint hot water), and dab lightly over the article. Raise the crochet up off the paper, to prevent it sticking as it dries. When dry, remove the pins and press the article lightly with a hot iron.

Mounting crochet to linen

Launder crochet first as explained and pin to the required shape, ensuring that all lines of the crochet are accurate. Place crochet in correct position on linen and secure with pins. Run a line of basting stitches on the linen following the outline of the crochet edges which are to be attached to the linen.

Remove crochet.

Turn under a small hem, with fold lying on line of basting stitches and slipstitch. Overcast crochet to the hem.

Or

Cut fabric ¼ in larger than required. Withdraw a thread ¼ in from edge all round and turn back a small hem. Attach thread to any corner, 3 dc into same place, dc closely all round, working into space of drawn thread having 3 dc into each corner, 1 ss into first dc. The crochet edging may be sewn to edge of dc, or edging worked into dc, according to instructions.

How to crochet

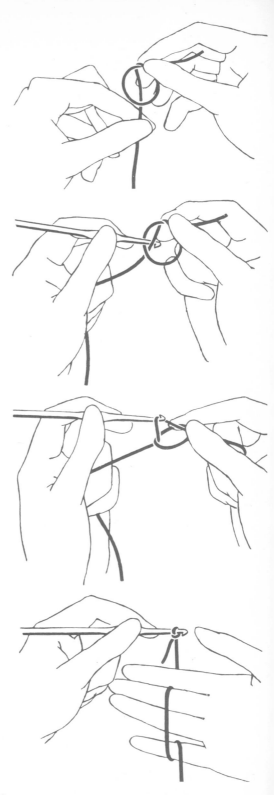

for the left handed

Left-handed people work from left to right.

The directions for each stitch apply to both right- and left-handed people.

For left-handed people only; place a pocket mirror to the left of each illustration and you will see the exact position in which you work reflected in the mirror, as shown in the illustrations on this page.

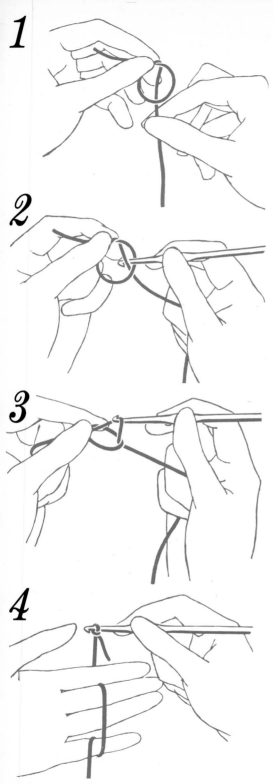

for the right handed

Right-handed people work from right to left.

Step 1, make a loop

1 Grasp thread near end between thumb and forefinger.
2 Make a loop by lapping long thread over short thread.
3 Hold loop in place between thumb and and forefinger *(fig 1)*.

Step 2

1 Take hold of broad bar of hook as you would a pencil. Bring middle finger for-forward to rest near tip of hook.
2 Insert hook through loop and under long thread. Catch long end of thread *(fig 2)*. Draw loop through.
3 Do not remove hook from thread.

Step 3

1 Pull short end and ball thread in opposite directions to bring loop close around the end of the hook, but not too tight *(fig 3)*.

Step 4

1 Loop thread round little finger, across palm and behind forefinger *(fig 4)*.

Step 5

1 Grasp hook and loop between thumb and forefinger.
2 Gently pull ball thread so that it lies around the fingers firmly but not tightly *(fig 5)*.
3 Catch knot of loop between thumb and forefinger.

Step 6

1 Adjust fingers as in *fig 6* – the middle finger is bent to regulate the tension; the ring and little fingers control the thread. The motion of the hook in one hand and the thread in the other hand should be free and even. Ease comes with practice.

Step 7

1 Pass your hook under thread and catch thread with hook. This is called 'thread over' *(fig 7)*.
2 Draw thread through loop on hook. This makes one chain (ch).

Step 8

1 Repeat Step 7 until you have as many chain stitches (ch sts) as you need – 1 loop always remains on the hook *(fig 8)*.
2 Always keep thumb and forefinger near stitch on which you are working.
3 Practice making chain stitches until they are even in size.

Slip stitch *abbreviation* – ss

Insert hook from the front under the 2 top threads of stitch to left of hook, catch thread with hook and draw through stitch and loop on hook *(fig 8a)*.

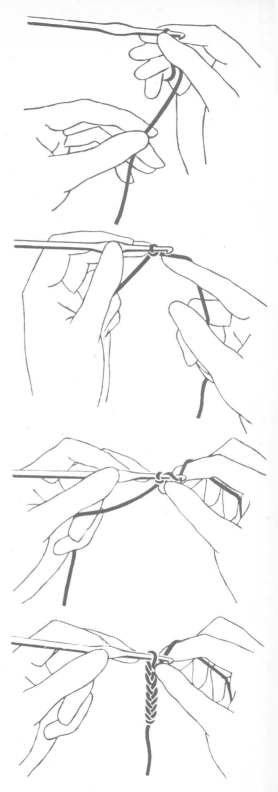

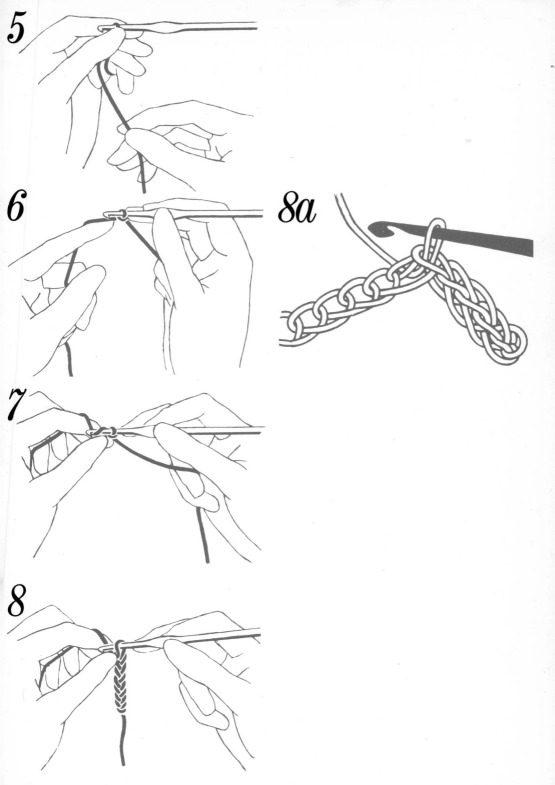

Rows of double crochet
abbreviation – dc

Note: In all crochet it is customary to pick up the 2 top loops (or threads) of each stitch as you work, unless otherwise specified.
Make a starting chain of 20 stitches for practice piece.

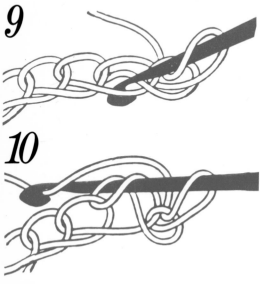
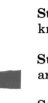

First Row (1st Row)

Step 1 Insert hook from the front under the 2 top threads of 2nd ch from hook *(fig 9)*.

Step 2 Catch thread with hook – this is known as 'thread over' *(fig 10)*.

Step 3 Draw thread through chain. There are 2 loops on hook *(fig 11)*.

Step 4 Thread over *(fig 12)* and draw through 2 loops – 1 loop remains on hook.

Step 5 You have now completed 1 double crochet (dc) *(fig 13)*.

Step 6 For next double crochet (dc) insert hook under 2 top threads of next ch and repeat Steps 2 to 6.

Step 7 Repeat Step 6 until you have made a double crochet (dc) in each ch.

Step 8 At end of row of double crochet, work 1 ch *(fig 14)*.
This 1 ch enables you to turn your work more easily but does not count as a stitch on next row.

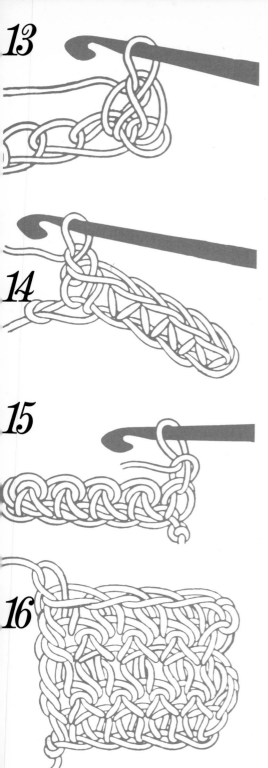

Step 9 Turn your work so that the reverse side is facing you *(fig 15)*.

Second Row (2nd Row)

Step 1 Insert hook from the front under the 2 top loops of first stitch (st) – the last dc made on previous row.

Step 2 Catch thread with hook ('thread over') and draw though st – 2 loops remain on hook.

Step 3 Thread over and draw through 2 loops – 1 loop remains on hook.

Step 4 For next double crochet (dc), insert hook from the front under the 2 top loops of next st and repeat Steps 2 and 3.

Step 5 Repeat Step 4 until you have made a double crochet (dc) into each dc, 1 ch and turn.

Step 6 Repeat Second Row (2nd Row) until you are familiar with this stitch. Fasten off *(fig 16)*.

How to 'Fasten off'

Step 1 Do not make a turning chain at end of last row.

Step 2 Cut thread about 3 in from work, bring loose end through the one remaining loop on hook and pull tightly *(fig 16)*.

Rows of half treble crochet
abbreviation – hlf tr

Note: When working rows of half treble (hlf tr) there is an extra loop on the wrong side directly below the 2 top loops of each hlf tr. Work only into the 2 top loops of each stitch. Make a starting chain of 20 stitches for practice piece.

First Row (1st Row)

Step 1 Pass hook under the thread of left hand (this is called 'thread over' *fig 17*).

Step 2 Insert hook from the front under the 2 top loops (or threads) of 3rd ch from hook.

Step 3 Thread over hook and draw loop through ch (3 loops on hook), thread over *(fig 18)*.

Step 4 Draw through all loops on hook – 1 loop remains on hook *(fig 19)*. A half treble (hlf tr) is now completed.

Step 5 For next half treble (hlf tr), thread over, insert hook from front under the 2 top threads of next ch.

Step 6 Repeat Steps 3 to 5 until you have made a half treble (hlf tr) in each ch.

Step 7 At end of row, 2 ch *(fig 20)* and turn.

The turning 2 ch does not count as a stitch on the following rows.

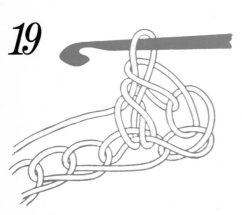

20

Second Row (2nd Row)

Step 1 Thread over hook, insert hook from front under the 2 top loops of first stitch (st) – the last hlf tr on previous row.

Step 2 Thread over hook and draw through stitch – there are 3 loops on hook, thread over and draw through all loops on hook.

Step 3 For next half treble (hlf tr), thread over hook, insert hook from the front under the 2 top loops of next stitch (st) and repeat Step 2.

Step 4 Repeat Step 3 until you have made a half treble (hlf tr) in each hlf tr, 2 ch and turn.

Step 5 Repeat Second Row (2nd Row) until you are familiar with this stitch. Fasten off at end of last row *(fig 16)*.

Rows of treble crochet
abbreviation – tr

Make a starting chain of 20 stitches for practice piece.

First Row (1st Row)

Step 1 Thread over, insert hook from the front under the 2 top threads of 4th ch from hook *(fig 21)*.

Step 2 Thread over and draw through stitch (st). There are now 3 loops on hook *(fig 22)*.

Step 3 Thread over and draw through 2 loops – 2 loops remain on hook *(fig 23)*.

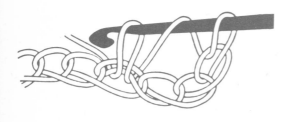

Step 4 Thread over again and draw through the 2 remaining loops – 1 loop remains on hook. One treble crochet (tr) is now completed *(fig 24)*.

Step 5 For next treble crochet (tr), thread over, insert hook from the front under the 2 top loops of next stitch (st) and repeat Steps 2 to 5 until you have made a treble crochet (tr) in each st.

Step 6 At end of row, 3 ch *(fig 25)* and turn. The 3 turning ch stand as 1 tr and count as the first st in the following row.

Second Row (2nd Row)

Step 1 Thread over, insert hook from the front under the 2 top loops of the 5th stitch from the hook (2nd stitch on previous row).

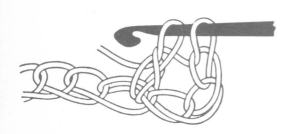

24

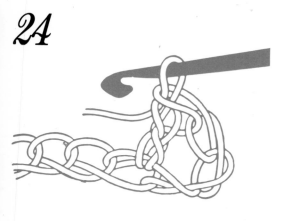

Step 2 Repeat steps 2 to 7 of first row. Repeat the second row until you are familiar with this stitch. Fasten off.

How to 'Turn your Work'

In rows of crochet a certain number of chain stitches are added at the end of each row to bring the work into position for the next row. Then the work is turned so that the reverse side is facing the worker. The number of turning chain depends upon the stitch with which you intend to begin the next row.

Turning Chain

25

$$
\begin{array}{r}
\text{dc} - 1\ \text{ch} \\
\text{hlf tr} - 2\ \text{ch} \\
\text{tr} - 3\ \text{ch} \\
\text{dbl tr} - 4\ \text{ch} \\
\text{trip tr} - 5\ \text{ch} \\
\text{quad tr} - 6\ \text{ch} \\
\text{quin tr} - 7\ \text{ch}
\end{array}
$$

The above list gives the number of turning ch for each type of stitch which would be used when the following row is to be commenced with the same stitch. When applied to any of the stitches bracketed, the turning ch also stands as the first stitch of the next row.

26

Rounds of double crochet

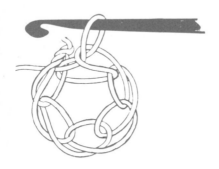

27

Step 1 Make a chain (ch) of 6 stitches (sts). Join with a slip stitch (ss) into 1st ch to form a ring *(figs 26 and 27)*.

Step 2 – 1st Row: Make 8 double crochet (dc) into ring *(fig 28)*. Place a safety pin in the last dc of 1st row to mark end of row. Move the safety pin to the last dc of the following rows.

Step 3 – 2nd Row: 2 double crochet (dc) into each dc of previous row – an increase made in each dc. There are 16 dc on row *(fig 29)*.

28

Step 4 – 3rd Row: * 2 double crochet (dc) into next dc – an increase made in last dc *(fig 29)*, 1 dc into next dc; repeat from * all round (24 dc on row).

Continue working in rows of double crochet as required, working increases wherever necessary in order to keep work flat and ending last row with 1 ss into each of next 2 dc. Fasten off.

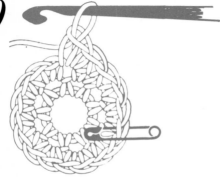

29

30

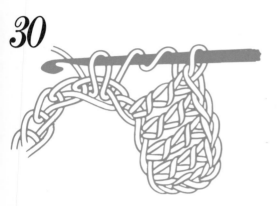

Double treble
abbreviation – dbl tr

Pass hook under the thread of left hand twice, insert hook into stitch to left of hook, thread over hook and draw through stitch (4 loops on hook) *(fig 30)*. Thread over hook and draw through 2 loops on hook, thread over hook and draw through other two loops on hook, thread over and draw through remaining 2 loops (1 loop remains on hook).

31

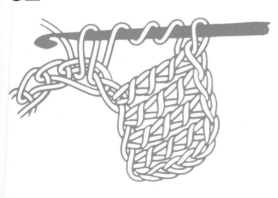

Triple treble
abbreviation – trip tr

Pass hook under the thread of left hand 3 times, insert hook into stitch to left of hook, thread over hook and draw through stitch (5 loops on hook) *(fig 31)*. Thread over hook and draw through 2 loops on hook, (thread over hook and draw through other 2 loops on hook) 3 times, 1 loop remains on hook.

Quadruple treble
abbreviation – quad tr

Pass hook under the thread of left hand 4 times and complete in same manner as trip tr until only 1 loop remains.

Quintuple treble
abbreviation – quin tr

Pass hook under the thread of left hand 5 times and complete in same manner as trip tr until only 1 loop remains.

32

Picot *abbreviation* – pl

Make a cha of 3, 4 or 5 sts according to
length of picot (p) desired, join ch to form
a ring working 1 dc into foundation or
first ch *(fig 32)*.

Clusters *abbreviation* – cl

Clusters may be worked in the following
ways:

(a) A cluster worked over a given number
of sts. Leaving the last loop of each on
hook, work 1 dbl tr into each of next 4 sts,
thread over hook and draw through all
loops on hook (a 4 dbl tr cluster made)
(fig 33).

33

(b) A cluster worked into one stitch.
Leaving the last loop of each stitch on
hook, work 3 or more stitches into same
stitch on previous row, thread over and
draw through all loops on hook *(fig 34)*.

(c) A cluster worked into loop or space.
Leaving the last loop of each stitch on
hook, work 3 or more stitches into space
or loop on previous row, thread over and
draw through all loops on hook *(fig 35)*.

34

35

36

Filet Crochet

The following four stitches are used mostly in Filet Crochet and are referred to as spaces, blocks, lacets and bars.

Space *abbreviation* – sp

Spaces are made with 2 ch, miss 2 stitches, 1 tr into next stitch *(fig 36)*.

Blocks and Spaces
abbreviation – blks and sps

37

Work 1 tr into each of next 4 stitches, 2 ch, miss 2 stitches, 1 tr into next stitch, 1 tr into each of next 3 stitches *(fig 37)*.

Bar and Lacet

(a) A bar consists of 5 ch, miss 5 stitches or a lacet, 1 tr into next stitch.

(b) A lacet consists of 3 ch, miss 2 stitches, 1 dc into next stitch, 3 ch, miss 2 stitches, 1 tr into next stitch *(fig 38)*.

38

Crochet for the home

Lampshade

Materials: 4 (50 grms) balls double knitting yarn.
No. 8 (4·00 mms) crochet hook.
Lampshade frame.

Measurements: To fit 14 ins diameter frame.

Abbreviations: Cl=cluster worked as follows:– yarn round hook, (insert hook in sp and draw a loop through, yarn round hook) 4 times, draw loop through all 9 loops on hook, then draw loop through last loop.

Make 12 ch, join with ss to form a ring.
1st round: 2 ch, 23 tr into ring, join with ss in 2nd of 2 ch.
2nd round: 2 ch, * 1 tr in next st, 2 tr in next st, rep from * ending with 1 tr in last st, 1 tr in base of 2 ch, 36 sts, join with ss in 2nd of 2 ch.
3rd round: 2 ch, * 1 tr in each of next 2 sts, 2 tr in next st, rep from * ending with 1 tr in each of last 2 sts, 1 tr in base of 2 ch, 48 sts, join with ss.
4th round: 2 ch, * 1 tr in each of next 3 sts, 2 tr in next st, rep from * ending with 1 tr in each of last 3 sts, 1 tr in base of 2 ch, 60 sts, join with ss.
5th round: 4 ch, 2 tr in same st as 4 ch, * 1 ch, miss 4 sts, (2 tr, 2 ch, 2 tr) in next st, rep from * ending with 1 ch, 1 tr in base of 4 ch, join with ss in 2nd of 4 ch.
6th round: Ss in 2 ch sp, 4 ch, 2 tr in 2 ch sp, * 1 ch, cl in 1 ch sp, 1 ch, (2 tr, 2 ch, 2 tr) in 2 ch sp, rep from * ending with 1 tr in 1st 2 ch sp, join with ss in 2nd of 4 ch.
7th round: Ss in 2 ch sp, 4 ch, 2 tr in 2 ch sp, * 1 ch, cl in top of cl, 1 ch, (2 tr, 2 ch, 2 tr) in 2 ch sp, rep from * ending with 1 tr in 1st 2 ch sp, join with ss in 2nd of 4 ch.
8th round: as 7th.
9th round: Ss in 2 ch sp, 4 ch, 2 tr in 2 ch sp, *

2 ch, cl in top of cl, 2 ch, (2 tr, 2 ch, 2 tr) in 2 ch sp, rep from * ending with 1 tr in 1st 2 ch sp, join with ss in 2nd of 4 ch.
10th round: as 9th.
11th round: Ss in 2 ch sp, 4 ch, 3 tr in 2 ch sp, * 2 ch, cl in top of cl, 2 ch, (3 tr, 2 ch, 3 tr) in 2 ch sp, rep from * ending with 2 tr in 1st 2 ch sp, join with ss in 2nd of 4 ch.
12th round: As 11th.
13th round: Ss in 2 ch sp, 4 ch, 3 tr in 2 ch sp, * 3 ch, cl in top of cl, 3 ch, (3 tr, 2 ch, 3 tr) in 2 ch sp, rep from * ending with 2 tr in 1st 2 ch sp, join with ss in 2nd of 4 ch.
14th round: As 13th.
15th round: Ss in 2 ch sp, 4 ch, 3 tr in 2 ch sp, * 4 ch, cl in top of cl, 4 ch, (3 tr, 2 ch, 3 tr) in 2 ch sp, rep from * ending with 2 tr in 1st 2 ch sp, join with ss in 2nd of 4 ch.
16th–22nd rounds: As 15th.

Work border

23rd round: * 1 dc in next tr, 1 hlf tr in each of next 2 tr, 3 tr in 4 ch sp, 1 tr in top of cl, 3 tr in 4 ch sp, 1 hlf tr in each of next 2 tr, 1 dc in next tr, 1 dc in 2 ch sp, rep from * all round, 168 sts, join with ss in 1st dc.
24th round: 2 ch, 1 tr in each st all round, join with ss.
25th and 26th rounds: As 24th.
27th round: 3 ch, miss 2 sts, * 1 tr in each of next 2 sts, 1 ch, miss 1 st, rep from * ending with 1 tr in last st, join with ss in 2nd of 3 ch. Fasten off.

To make up

Place shade on frame and pin in position with shell panels positioned over spokes of frame and lower edge of frame level with 1st row of border. Sew lower edge of frame to 1st row of border on wrong side.
Cut 280 16 ins lengths of yarn. Using 5 strands together each time, double yarn and knot into each ch sp along lower edge as illustrated. Trim fringes.

Early morning set

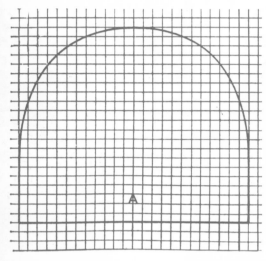

A – Front and Back *(cut 2)*

Note: All patterns made from diagrams:
1 square=$\frac{1}{2}$ in.

Materials: Coats Mercer-Crochet no. 20
(20 grms).
3 balls.
This model is worked in shade 538 (Marigold),
but any other shade of Mercer-Crochet may be
used.
Milward steel crochet hook 1·25 (no. 3), or size
to fit tension (gauge).
$\frac{3}{4}$ yd Heavy Green linen 48 ins wide.
Tea cosy pad $10\frac{1}{2} \times 9$ ins.

Tension (gauge):
Size of motif=2 ins square.
Edging = 44 ins long approximately.
Measurements:
Tea cosy = 11×9 ins.
Tray cloth = 20×14 ins.
Napkin = 12 ins square.

Suitable fabric
Old bleach linen L2705 (Moss Green).

Tea cosy

First motif
Commence with 10 ch, join with a ss to form a
ring.
1st row: 3 ch, 4 tr into ring, remove loop from
hook, insert hook into 3rd of 3 ch then into
dropped loop and draw loop through (a starting popcorn st made), * 3 ch, 5 tr into ring,
remove loop from hook, insert hook into first
tr of treble group, then into dropped loop
and draw loop through (a popcorn st made);
repeat from * 6 times more, 3 ch, 1 ss into first
loop.
2nd row: Into first loop work a starting pop--
corn st 3 ch and a popcorn st, * 3 ch, into next
loop work a popcorn st 3 ch and a popcorn st;

repeat from * ending with 3 ch, 1 ss into first loop.

3rd row: 1 dc into same loop as ss, 6 ch, 1 dc into 6th ch from hook, 7 ch, 1 dc into last dc, 5 ch, 1 dc into last dc, (8 ch, 1 dc into last dc, 5 ch, 1 dc into last dc) 3 times, 7 ch, 1 dc into last dc, 5 ch, 1 dc into last dc, 1 ch, 1 dc into same 3 ch loop (corner completed), * 3 dc into next loop, 1 dc into next loop, 6 ch, 1 dc into 6th ch from hook, 3 ch, remove loop from hook, insert hook into last 7 ch loop made on corner and draw dropped loop through, 3 ch, 1 dc into last dc, 6 ch, 1 dc into last dc, 7 ch, 1 dc into last dc, 5 ch, 1 dc into last dc, 1 ch, 1 dc into same 3 ch loop (side completed), 3 dc into next loop, 1 dc into next loop, 6 ch, 1 dc into 6th ch from hook, 3 ch, remove loop from hook, insert hook into last 7 ch loop made on side and draw dropped loop through, 3 ch, 1 dc into last dc, complete corner as before; repeat from * 3 times more omitting corner at end of last repeat and joining last 7 ch loop on last side to first 7 ch loop on first corner, 1 ss into first dc. Fasten off.

Second motif
Work as first motif for 2 rows.

3rd row: 1 dc into same loop as ss, 6 ch, 1 dc into 6th ch from hook, 7 ch, 1 dc into last dc, 5 ch, 1 dc into last dc, 8 ch, 1 dc into last dc, 5 ch, 1 dc into last dc, 4 ch, 1 ss into corresponding loop on first motif, 4 ch, 1 dc into last dc, 5 ch, 1 dc into last dc, 4 ch, 1 ss into corresponding loop on first motif, 4 ch, 1 dc into last dc, 5 ch, 1 dc into last dc, 7 ch, 1 dc into last dc, 5 ch, 1 dc into last dc, 1 ch, 1 dc into same 3 ch loop, 3 dc into next loop, 1 dc into next loop, 6 ch, 1 dc into 6th ch from hook, 3 ch, remove loop from hook, insert hook into 7 ch loop made on corner and draw dropped loop through, 3 ch, 1 dc into last dc, 3 ch, 1 ss into corresponding loop on first motif, 3 ch, 1 dc into last dc, 7 ch, 1 dc into last dc, 5 ch, 1 dc into last dc, 1 ch, 1 dc into same 3 ch loop, 3 dc into next loop, 1 dc into next loop, 6 ch, 1 dc into 6th ch from hook, 3 ch, remove loop from hook, insert hook into 7 ch loop made on side and draw dropped loop through, 3 ch, 1 dc into last dc, (5 ch, 1 dc into last dc, 4 ch, 1 ss into corresponding loop on first motif, 4 ch, 1 dc into last dc) twice, 5 ch, 1 dc into last dc, and complete as first motif.

Make 9 more motifs joining each as second motif was joined to first (to form a strip) and joining last motif to first motif as before.

Tray cloth

Make 10 motifs joining each as second motif was joined to first.

Eleventh motif
Work motif as before, joining to last motif leaving one corner free at outside edge. Make 5 more motifs joining as before.
Work other two sides to correspond.

Napkin

Make one motif as first motif.

Edging
6 ch, 1 dc into 6th ch from hook, * 8 ch, 1 dc into last dc, 5 ch, 1 dc into last dc; repeat from * for 44 ins or length required to go round napkin. Fasten off.
Damp and pin out to measurements.

To make up
Tea cosy
Place fabric wrong sides together and machine stitch round curved edge taking $\frac{1}{2}$ in seam. Trim and turn to right side. Turn in 1 in across lower edge and sew neatly in position. Sew motifs across lower edge as shown in illustration.

Tray cloth
Cut 1 piece of fabric $21\frac{1}{2} \times 15\frac{1}{2}$ ins. Turn in $\frac{1}{2}$ in hems, mitre corners and slipstitch in position. Sew motifs in position to linen.

Napkin
Cut 1 piece of fabric $13\frac{1}{2}$ ins square. Turn in $\frac{1}{2}$ in hems, mitre corners and slipstitch in position.
Sew motif to one corner and sew edging to edge of napkin omitting corner with motif.

Motif trolley cloth

for detail, see page 34

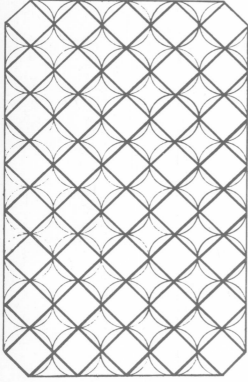

◇ *Motif*   ◇ *Filling*   △ *Half Filling*

Materials: Coats Mercer-Crochet no. 20 (20 grms).
5 balls.
This model is worked in shade 962 (Dk Buttercup), but any other shade of Mercer-Crochet may be used.
Milward steel crochet hook 1·25 (no. 3) or size to fit tension (gauge).

Measurements: Size of motif=3 ins across.

Size of cloth=16 × 25 ins.

First motif

Commence with 10 ch, join with a ss to form a ring.
1st row: 3 ch, 23 tr into ring, 1 ss into 3rd of 3 ch.
2nd row: 3 ch, leaving the last loop of each on hook work 2 tr into same place as ss, thread over and draw through all loops on hook (a 2 tr cluster made), 4 ch, a 3 tr cluster into same place * 5 ch, miss 2 tr, 1 dc into next tr, 5 ch miss 2 tr, into next tr work a 3 tr cluster 4 ch and a 3 tr cluster; repeat from * omitting a 3 tr cluster 4 ch and a 3 tr cluster at end of last repeat, 1 ss into first cluster.
3rd row: 1 ss into next loop, 3 ch, into same loop work a 2 tr cluster (3 ch, a 3 tr cluster) twice, * 4 ch, 1 dc into next sp, 1 dc into next dc, 1 dc into next sp, 4 ch, into next loop work (a 3 tr cluster, 3 ch) twice and a 3 tr cluster; repeat from * omitting (a 3 tr cluster, 3 ch) twice and a 3 tr cluster at end of last repeat, 1 ss into first cluster.
4th row: 1 ss into next loop, 3 ch, into same loop work a 2 tr cluster 3 ch and a 3 tr cluster, * 3 ch, into next loop work a 3 tr cluster 3 ch and a 3 tr cluster, 6 ch, leaving the last loop of each on hook work 1 dbl tr into each of next 2 sps, thread over and draw through all

loops on hook (a joint dbl tr made), 6 ch, into next loop work a 3 tr cluster 3 ch and a 3 tr cluster; repeat from * omitting 6 ch a 3 tr cluster 3 ch and a 3 tr cluster at end of last repeat, 3 ch, 1 tr into first cluster.

5th row: 1 dc into loop just formed, * 5 ch, 1 dc into next loop, 3 ch, into next loop work 2 tr 3 ch and 2 tr (a shell made), 3 ch, 1 dc into next loop, 5 ch, 1 dc into next loop, 3 ch, a shell into next joint dbl tr, 3 ch, 1 dc into next loop; repeat from * omitting 1 dc at end of last repeat, 1 ss into first dc. Fasten off.

Second motif

Work as first motif for 4 rows.

5th row: 1 dc into loop just formed, 5 ch, 1 dc into next loop, 3 ch, 2 tr into next loop, 1 ch, 1 dc into corresponding loop on first motif, 1 ch, 2 tr into same loop on second motif and complete as first motif.

Make 8 rows of 5 motifs, joining each as second motif was joined to first, placing as shown on diagram.

Filling

Commence with 7 ch, join with a ss to form a ring.

1st row: 3 ch, 15 tr into ring, 1 ss into 3rd of 3 ch.

2nd row: 3 ch, into same place as ss work a 2 tr cluster 3 ch and a 3 tr cluster, * 3 ch, miss 1 tr, 1 tr into next tr, 3 ch, miss 1 tr, into next tr work a 3 tr cluster 3 ch and a 3 tr cluster; repeat from * omitting a 3 tr cluster 3 ch and a 3 tr cluster at end of last repeat, 1 ss into next cluster.

3rd row: 1 dc into same place as ss, 1 dc into next loop, 2 ch, 1 ss into any free shell between joinings, * 2 ch, 1 dc into same place on filling, 1 dc into next cluster, 4 ch, a 3 dbl tr cluster into next tr, 6 ch, 1 ss into next joining of motifs, 6 ch, a 3 dbl tr cluster into same place on filling, 4 ch, 1 dc into next cluster, 1 dc into next loop, 2 ch, 1 ss into next free shell; repeat from * omitting 2 dc at end of last repeat, 1 ss into first dc. Fasten off. Fill in all spaces between four motifs in this manner.

Half filling

Commence with 7 ch, join with a ss to form a ring.

1st row: 3 ch, 15 tr into ring, 1 ss into 3rd of 3 ch.

2nd row: 6 ch, * miss 1 tr, into next tr work a 3 tr cluster 3 ch and a 3 tr cluster, * * 3 ch, miss 1 tr, 1 tr into next tr, 3 ch; repeat from * to * *, 6 ch, miss 1 tr, 1 ss into each of next 8 tr and into 3 ch of 6 ch.

3rd row: 4 ch, a 2 dbl tr cluster into same place as last ss, 6 ch, 1 ss into free shell on motif as marked by * on diagram, * 6 ch, a 3 dbl tr cluster into same place on half filling, 4 ch, 1 dc into next cluster on half filling, 1 dc into next loop, 2 ch, 1 ss into next shell on motif, 2 ch, 1 dc into same place on half filling, 1 dc into next cluster, 4 ch, * * a 3 dbl tr cluster into next tr, 6 ch, 1 ss into joining of motifs; repeat from * to * *, a 3 dbl tr cluster into 4th of 6 ch on half filling, 6 ch, 1 ss into next shell on motif, 6 ch, a 3 dbl tr cluster into same place on half filling. Fasten off.

Fill in all spaces round outer edge in this manner.

Edging

1st row: Attach thread to sp of free shell at any corner, 3 ch, into same sp work 1 tr (2 ch and 2 tr) twice, * * (5 ch, 1 dc into next dc) twice, 5 ch, 1 dc into sp of next shell, * 5 ch, 1 dc into next sp, 5 ch, 1 dc into next cluster, 5 ch, 1 dc into same place as base of cluster, 5 ch, miss 3 tr, 1 dc into next tr, 5 ch, 1 dc into same place as base of next cluster, 5 ch, 1 dc into top of cluster, 5 ch, 1 dc into next sp, 5 ch, 1 dc into sp of next shell; repeat from * along side, ending with (5 ch, 1 dc into next dc) twice, 5 ch, into sp of shell at corner work (2 tr, 2 ch) twice and 2 tr; repeat from * * omitting corner at end of last repeat, 1 ss into 3rd of 3 ch.

2nd row: 1 ss into next tr and next sp, 3 ch, 1 tr into same sp, 2 ch, 2 tr into same sp, * into next sp work 2 tr 2 ch and 2 tr, into each 5 ch loop along side work 1 dc 1 hlf tr 1 tr 2 ch 1 tr 1 hlf tr and 1 dc, into first sp at next corner work 2 tr 2 ch and 2 tr; repeat from * omitting 2 tr 2 ch and 2 tr at end of last repeat, 1 ss into 3rd of 3 ch. Fasten off. Damp and pin out to measurements.

Cheval set

Materials: Coats Mercer-Crochet no. 20
(20 grms).
2 balls.
This model is worked in shade 621 (Lt. French
Blue), but any other shade of Mercer-Crochet
may be used.
Milward steel crochet hook 1·25 (no. 3), or size
to fit tension (gauge).

Tension (gauge): First 3 rows = 1⅝ ins in
diameter.

Measurements: Centrepiece = 10½ ins
diameter. Small Mat = 5½ ins diameter.

Centrepiece
Commence with 5 ch.
1st row: 15 dbl tr into 5th ch from hook, 1 ss
into 5th of 5 ch.
2nd row: 4 ch, leaving the last loop of each on
hook work 2 dbl tr into same place as ss,
thread over and draw through all loops on
hook (a 2 dbl tr cluster made), * 4 ch, a 3 dbl
tr cluster into next dbl tr; repeat from * ending with 4 ch, 1 ss into first cluster.
3rd row: Ss to centre of first loop, 1 dc into
same loop, * 4 ch, 1 dc into next loop; repeat
from * ending with 2 ch, 1 hlf tr into first dc.
4th row: 1 dc into loop just formed, * 5 ch,
1 dc into next loop; repeat from * ending with
2 ch, 1 tr into first dc.
5th row: 1 dc into loop just formed, * 1 ch,
into next dc work 2 tr 1 ch and 2 tr, 1 ch, 1 dc
into next loop; repeat from * omitting 1 dc at
end of last repeat, 1 ss into first dc.
6th row: 3 ch, into same place as ss work
1 tr 1 ch and 2 tr, * 1 ch, miss 2 tr, 1 dc into
next sp, 1 ch, into next dc work 2 tr 1 ch and
2 tr; repeat from * omitting 2 tr 1 ch and 2 tr at
end of last repeat, 1 ss into 3rd of 3 ch.
7th row: 1 ss into next tr, * 1 dc into next sp,

3 ch, 1 tr into next dc, 3 ch, miss 2 tr; repeat
from * ending with 1 ss into first dc.
8th row: 1 ss into next ch, 1 dc into same sp,
* 4 ch, 1 dc into next sp; repeat from * ending
with 4 ch, 1 ss into first dc.
9th row: 1 ss into each of first 2 ch, 1 dc into
same loop, * 5 ch, 1 dc into next loop; repeat
from * ending with 2 ch, 1 tr into first dc.
10th row: 1 dc into loop just formed, * 5 ch,
1 dc into next loop; repeat from * ending with
2 ch, 1 tr into first dc.
11th row: 1 dc into loop just formed, * 4 ch, a
4 dbl tr cluster into next dc, 4 ch, 1 dc into next
loop; repeat from * omitting 4 ch and 1 dc at
end of last repeat, 1 ch, 1 tr into first dc.
12th row: 1 dc into loop just formed, * 3 ch,
1 dc into next loop; repeat from * ending with
3 ch, 1 ss into first dc.
13th row: 1 ss into next ch, 1 dc into same
loop, * 4 ch, 1 dc into next loop; repeat from *
ending with 4 ch, 1 ss into first dc.
14th and 15th rows: As 13th row.
16th row: 1 ss into next ch, 1 dc into same
loop, * 5 ch, 1 dc into next loop; repeat from *
ending with 2 ch, 1 tr into first dc.
17th row: 1 dc into loop just formed, * 5 ch,
1 dc into next loop; repeat from * ending with
2 ch, 1 tr into first dc.
18th to 23rd row: As 17th row.
24th row: As 5th row.
25th row: As 6th row.
26th row: 1 ss into next tr, * 1 dc into next sp,
1 ch, into next dc work 2 tr 1 ch and 2 tr, 1 ch,
miss 2 tr; repeat from * ending with 1 ss into
first dc.
27th row: As 6th row.
28th row: 1 ss into next tr, 1 dc into next sp,
* 6 ch, miss 4 tr, 1 dc into next sp; repeat from
* ending with 3 ch, 1 tr into first dc.
29th row: As 5th row.
30th row: As 6th row.
31st row: As 26th row. Fasten off.

Small mat (make 2)
Work as centre piece for 10 rows.
11th row: As 11th row of centrepiece ending
with 4 ch, 1 ss into first dc.
12th row: 1 ss into each of next 4 ch and into
next cluster, 1 dc into same cluster, * 6 ch,
1 dc into next cluster; repeat from * ending
with 3 ch, 1 tr into first dc.
13th to 15th row: As 29th to 31st row of
centrepiece.
Damp and pin out to measurements.

36

Motif runner

8th row: 1 ss into each of next 3 ch, 3 ch, leaving the last loop of each on hook work 2 tr into loop, thread over and draw through all loops on hook (a cluster made), 3 ch, 1 dc into next dc, * 3 ch, a 3 tr cluster into next loop, 3 ch, 1 dc into next dc; repeat from * working last dc into same place as ss of previous row, 3 ch, 1 ss into top of first cluster.

9th row: (8 ch, 1 ss into same place as last ss) 3 times, * 5 ch, into next cluster work 1 ss 4 ch and 1 ss, 5 ch, into next cluster work (1 ss, 8 ch) 3 times and 1 ss; repeat from * omitting (8 ch, 1 ss), 3 times and working last ss into base of first 8 ch. Fasten off.

Second motif

Work as first motif for 8 rows.

9th row: 8 ch, 1 ss into same place as last ss, * 4 ch, 1 ss into corresponding 8 ch loop on first motif, 4 ch, 1 ss into same place on second motif, 4 ch, 1 ss into next 8 ch loop on first motif, 4 ch, 1 ss into same place on second motif, * 5 ch, 1 ss into next cluster, 2 ch, 1 ss into corresponding 4 ch loop on first motif, 2 ch, 1 ss into same place on second motif, 5 ch, 1 ss into next cluster; repeat from * to * once more, 8 ch, 1 ss into same place on second motif, complete as for first motif.

Make 3 rows of 10 motifs, joining adjacent sides as second motif was joined to first motif, leaving 3 loops free between joinings.

Filling

Commence with 8 ch, join with a ss to form a ring.

1st row: 12 dc into ring, 1 ss into first dc.

2nd row: 1 dc into same place as ss, 6 ch, 1 ss into any free loop between joinings of motifs, 6 ch, 1 dc into next dc on filling, * 6 ch, 1 ss into next free loop on motif, 6 ch, 1 dc into next dc on filling; repeat from * 10 times more, omitting 1 dc at end of last repeat, 1 ss into first dc. Fasten off.

Fill in all spaces between motifs in same manner. Damp and pin out to measurements.

Alternative suggestion

Teacloth

Measurements: 36 ins square (12 motifs × 12 motifs).

14 motifs, 10 fillings can be worked from 1 ball no. 20.

Materials: Coats Mercer-Crochet no. 20 (20 grms).
3 balls.
This model is worked in shade 521 (Jade), but any other shade of Mercer-Crochet may be used.
Milward steel crochet hook 1·25 (no. 3), or size to fit tension (gauge).

Size of motif: 3 ins diameter approximately.

Measurements: 9 × 30 ins. approximately.

First motif

Commence with 10 ch, join with a ss to form a ring.

1st row: 16 dc into ring, 1 ss into first dc.

2nd row: 1 dc into same place as ss, * 5 ch, miss 1 dc, 1 dc into next dc; repeat from * omitting 1 dc at end of last repeat, 1 ss into first dc.

3rd row: 1 ss into each of next 3 sts, 1 dc into loop, * 5 ch, 1 dc into next loop; repeat from * omitting 1 dc at end of last repeat, 1 ss into first dc.

4th row: 1 ss into each of next 3 sts, 1 dc into loop, * 7 ch, 1 dc into next loop; repeat from * omitting 1 dc at end of last repeat, 1 ss into first dc.

5th row: 2 ch, * 9 hlf tr into next loop, 1 hlf tr into next dc; repeat from * omitting 1 hlf tr at end of last repeat, 1 ss into 2nd of 2 ch.

6th row: 1 dc into same place as ss, * 5 ch, miss 4 hlf tr, 1 dc into next hlf tr; repeat from * omitting 1 dc at end of last repeat, 1 ss into first dc.

7th row: 1 ss into each of the next 3 ch, 1 dc into loop, * 5 ch, 1 dc into next loop; repeat from * omitting 1 dc at end of last repeat, 1 ss into first dc.

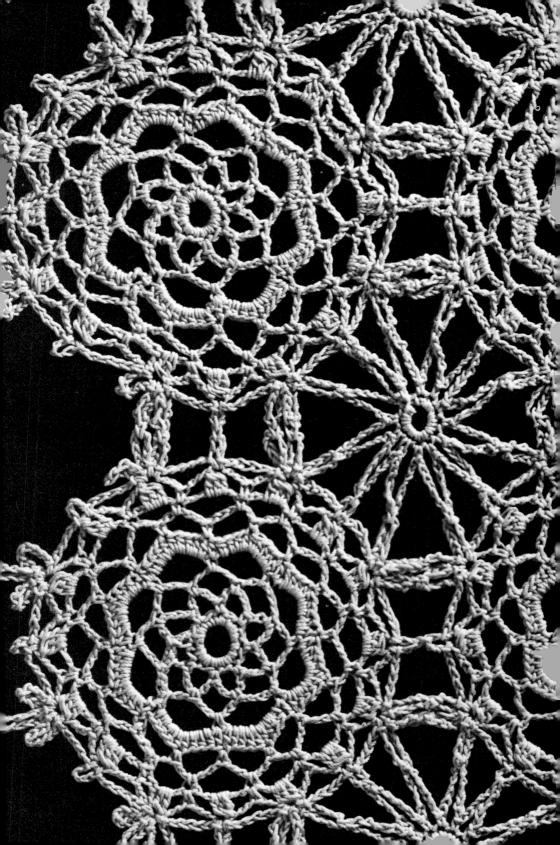

Motif teacloth

Materials: Coats Mercer-Crochet no. 20 (20 grms).
16 balls.
This model is worked in shade 8918 (Lt. Coral Pink), but any other shade of Mercer-Crochet may be used.
Milward steel crochet hook 1·25 (no. 3), or size to fit tension (gauge).

Size of motif: 3 ins square.

Measurements: 36 × 36 ins.

First motif

Commence with 7 ch, join with a ss to form a ring.
1st row: 4 ch, 23 dbl tr into ring, 1 ss into 4th of 4 ch.
2nd row: 9 ch, 1 ss into 3rd of 9 ch, * 7 ch, miss 2 dbl tr, 1 trip tr into next dbl tr, 6 ch, 1 ss into top of last trip tr, 7 ch, miss 2 dbl tr, 1 tr into next dbl tr, 6 ch, 1 ss into top of last tr; repeat from * ending with 7 ch, miss 2 dbl tr, 1 ss into 3rd of 9 ch.
3rd row: 1 ss into first ch of 6 ch loop, 1 ss into loop, 5 ch, into same loop work (2 dbl tr 2 tr 6 ch 1 ss into top of last tr 1 tr 2 dbl tr and 1 trip tr), * into next 6 ch loop work (2 trip tr 3 dbl tr 2 trip tr 6 ch 1 ss into top of last trip tr 1 trip tr 3 dbl tr and 2 trip tr), into next 6 ch loop work (1 trip tr 2 dbl tr 2 tr 6 ch 1 ss into top of last tr 1 tr 2 dbl tr and 1 trip tr): repeat from * omitting 1 trip tr 2 dbl tr 2 tr 6 ch loop 1 tr 2 dbl tr and 1 trip tr at end of last repeat, 1 ss into 5th of 5 ch.
4th row: 1 ss into each of next 4 sts, 1 ss into first ch of 6 ch loop, 1 ss into 6 ch loop, 9 ch, into same loop work (1 dbl tr, 4 ch) 3 times and 1 trip tr, * into next 6 ch loop work 1 trip tr 4 ch (1 dbl tr, 4 ch) 5 times and 1 trip tr, into next 6 ch loop work 1 trip tr 4 ch (1 dbl tr, 4 ch) 3 times and 1 trip tr; repeat from * ending with (1 dbl tr, 4 ch) 5 times and 1 trip tr, 1 ss into 5th of 9 ch.
5th row: 5 dc into each 4 ch sp, 1 ss into first dc. Fasten off.

Second motif

Work as first motif for 4 rows.
5th row: 5 dc into each of next 7 loops, * (3 dc into next loop, 1 ss into centre dc of corresponding loop on first motif, 2 dc into same loop on second motif) twice, 5 dc into each of next 2 loops on second motif; repeat from * twice more, complete as for first motif. Fasten off.
Make 12 rows of 12 motifs joining each as second was joined to first.
Damp and pin out to measurements.

Alternative suggestion:

Trolley Mat

Measurements: 15 × 24 ins (5 motifs × 8 motifs).
9 motifs can be worked from 1 ball no. 20.

Chairback and armrests

Materials: Coats Mercer-Crochet no. 40
(20 grms).
3 balls selected colour.
Milward steel crochet hook 1·00 (no. 4).
(If your crochet is loose use a size finer hook,
if tight use a size larger hook.)

Tension: 5 sps and 5 rows = 1 in.

Measurements: Chairback, $14\frac{1}{2} \times 15\frac{1}{5}$ ins.
Armrests, 8×11 ins.

Chairback

Make a chain about 20 ins long (17 ch sts to
1 in).
1st row: 1 tr into 4th ch from hook, 1 tr into
each of next 227 ch, cut off remaining ch, 3 ch,
turn.
2nd row: Miss first tr, 1 tr into each of next
3 tr (blk made over blk), 2 ch, miss 2 tr,
1 tr into next tr (sp made over blk), 15 sps, 1 tr
into each of next 3 tr (blk made over blk), 4
sps, 1 blk, 12 sps, 1 blk, 2 sps. Diagram shows
half of row. To make second half of row, follow
diagram, working back from centre of row to
beginning, 3 ch, turn.
3rd row: 1 blk, 2 ch, 1 tr into next tr (sp made
over sp), 14 sps, 1 blk, 6 sps, 1 blk, 10 sps, 1 blk,
3 sps and work other half of row as before, following diagram.
4th row: 1 blk, 14 sps, 1 blk, 8 sps, 1 blk, 8 sps,
1 blk, 4 sps, work other half of row as before,
following diagram.
Follow diagram, working second half of each
row as before, until 11 rows are completed,
3 ch, turn.
12th row: 1 blk, 8 sps, 1 blk, 3 ch, miss 2 sts,
1 dc into next st, 3 ch, miss 2 sts, 1 tr into next
tr (lacet made), 1 blk, 4 sps, 2 blks, 2 sps, 2 blks,
4 sps, 1 blk, 1 lacet, 1 blk, 4 sps, 2 blks, 1 sp.
Work other half of row as before, 3 ch, turn.

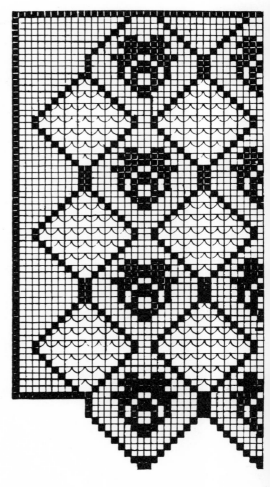

☐ *Space*

■ *Block*

⊓ *Bar*

⋈ *Lacet*

42

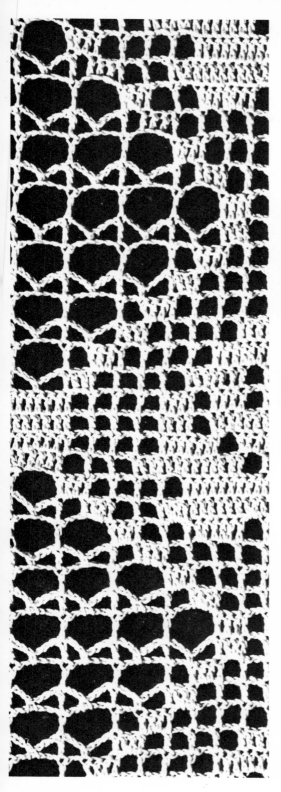

13th row: 1 blk, 7 sps, 1 blk, 1 sp, 5 ch, 1 tr into next tr (bar made), 1 sp, 1 blk, 4 sps, 4 blks, 4 sps, 1 blk, 1 sp, 1 bar, 1 sp, 1 blk, 4 sps, 2 blks. Work other half of row as before, 3 ch, turn.

14th row: 1 blk, 6 sps, 1 blk, 3 lacets, 1 blk, 4 sps, 2 blks, 4 sps, 1 blk, 3 lacets, 1 blk, 4 sps, 1 blk. Work other half of row as before, 3 ch, turn.

Follow diagram until 62 rows are completed. Fasten off.

Points

1st row: Attach thread to first tr of 12th blk on last row, 3 ch and complete blk, 4 sps, 2 blks, 1 sp, 2 blks, 1 sp, 2 blks, 4 sps, 2 blks, 4 sps, 2 blks, 1 sp, 1 blk, work second half as before, 3 ch, turn.

2nd row: Follow diagram across, 3 ch, turn.

3rd row: Follow diagram. Do not ch to turn.

4th row: 1 ss into each of next 3 tr (blk decreased), 3 ch and complete blk, 4 sps, 2 blks, 2 sps, 2 blks, 4 sps, 1 blk, turn.

Follow diagram to end. Work other two points same as this at corresponding places.

Armrest *make 2*

Follow diagram for Armrest. Damp and press.

43

Filet doily

Materials: Coats Mercer-Crochet no. 10
(20 grms).
3 balls.
This model is worked in 442 (Mid Buttercup),
but any other shade of Mercer-Crochet may be
used.
Milward steel crochet 1·50 (no. 2½), or size to
fit tension (gauge).

Tension (gauge): 4 sps and 4 rows=1 in.

Measurement: 16 ins diameter.

Commence with 32 ch.
1st row: 1 tr into 8th ch from hook, * 2 ch,

miss 2 ch, 1 tr into next ch; repeat from * 7
times more (9 sps made), 16 ch, turn.
2nd row: 1 tr into 8th ch from hook, (2 ch,
miss 2 ch, 1 tr into next ch) twice, 2 ch, miss 2
ch, 1 tr into next tr (4 extension sps made at
beginning of row), * 2 tr into next sp, 1 tr into
next tr (blk made over sp); repeat from * 7
times more, 2 tr into next sp, 1 tr into top of
turning ch, 5 ch, 1 tr into same place as last tr,
* 5 ch, turn, 1 tr into 3rd of previous 5 ch;
repeat from last * twice more (4 extension sps
made at end of row), 13 ch, turn.
3rd row: 1 tr into 8th ch from hook, 2 ch, miss
2 ch, 1 tr into next ch, 2 ch, 1 tr into top of next
tr (3 extension sps made), 4 blks, * 2 ch, miss
2 tr, 1 tr into next tr (sp made over blk); repeat
from * 8 times more, 4 blks, 5 ch, 1 tr into same
place as last tr, (5 ch, turn, 1 tr into 3rd of previous 5 ch) twice (3 extension sps made), turn,
1 ss into each of next 4 sts, 10 ch, turn.

Follow diagram from 4th row to top (centre
row). Turn diagram and omitting centre row
work back to beginning, decreasing sps
instead of increasing. (To decrease—omit
turning ch at end of row, turn and ss along
4 sts, 5 ch). Fasten off. Damp and press.

Centre row

4th Row

Commence ch here ⟶

Key
☐ *Space*
■ *Block*

Curtain edging

Materials: Coats Mercer-Crochet no. 40
(20 grms). 2 balls.
This model is worked in White, but any other
shade of Mercer-Crochet may be used.
$2\frac{1}{2}$ yds cotton, 36 ins wide, as in illustration.
Milward steel crochet hook 1·00 (no. 4), or
size to fit tension (gauge).
The above quantity is sufficient for 2 curtains,
finished size $36\frac{1}{2} \times 44\frac{1}{2}$ ins. approximately.
Depth of edging: $1\frac{1}{2}$ ins.
Cut material in half and make $\frac{1}{4}$ in hems along
three sides and $1\frac{1}{4}$ ins hem along top of each
curtain.
Make a chain to measure slightly longer than
length of one side and lower edge of curtain.
1st row: 1 dc into 2nd ch from hook, 1 dc into
each of next 7 ch, * 3 ch, miss 3 ch, 1 dc into
each of next 8 ch; repeat from * until there is
sufficient to go along lower edge of curtain,
ending with 8 dc (corner), 3 ch, 1 dc into same
place as last dc, 1 dc into each of next 7 ch, * 3
ch, miss 3 ch, 1 dc into each of next 8 ch;
repeat from last * until there is sufficient to go
along side of curtain, ending with 8 dc, cut off
remaining ch, 4 ch, turn.
2nd row: Miss first dc, 1 dbl tr into each of
next 7 dc, * 1 ch, 1 dbl tr into next 3 ch sp, 1 ch,
1 dbl tr into each of next 8 dc; repeat from * to
corner, 3 ch, 1 dbl tr into 3 ch loop, 3 ch, 1 dbl
tr into each of next 8 dc, * 1 ch, 1 dbl tr into
next 3 ch sp, 1 ch, 1 dbl tr into each of next 8
dc; repeat from last * to end of row, 1 ch, turn.
3rd row: 1 dc into each of first 7 dbl tr, * 2 ch,
1 dc into next sp, 1 dc into next dbl tr, 1 dc into
next sp, 2 ch, miss 1 dbl tr, 1 dc into each of
next 6 dbl tr; repeat from * to corner, 4 ch, 1 dc
into next sp, 1 dc into next dbl tr, 1 dc into
next sp, 4 ch, miss 1 dbl tr, 1 dc into each of
next 6 dbl tr, * 2 ch, 1 dc into next sp, 1 dc into
next dbl tr, 1 dc into next sp, 2 ch, miss 1 dbl tr,
1 dc into each of next 6 dbl tr; repeat from last

* to end of row, 1 dc into top of turning ch,
5 ch, turn.
4th row: Miss first 2 dc, * 1 tr into each of
next 4 dc, 3 ch, 1 dc into next 2 ch sp, 4 ch, 1 dc
into next 2 ch sp, 3 ch, miss 1 dc; repeat from *
to corner, 1 tr into each of next 4 dc, 4 ch, 1 dc
into next 4 ch sp, 5 ch, 1 dc into next 4 ch sp, 4
ch, miss 1 dc, 1 tr into each of next 4 dc, * 3 ch,
1 dc into next 2 ch sp, 4 ch, 1 dc into next 2 ch
sp, 3 ch, miss 1 dc, 1 tr into each of next 4 dc;
repeat from last * ending with 2 ch, miss 1 dc,
1 tr into next dc, 6 ch, turn.
5th row: Miss 1 tr 2 ch and 1 tr, 1 dbl tr into
each of next 2 tr, * 2 ch, leaving the last loop of
each on hook work 3 trip tr into next 4 ch
loop, thread over and draw through all loops
on hook (a trip tr cluster made), 4 ch, into
same loop work 3 trip tr clusters with 4 ch between each, 2 ch, miss 1 tr, 1 dbl tr into each of
next 2 tr; repeat from * to corner, 2 ch, 5 trip tr
clusters with 4 ch between each into next 5 ch
loop, * 2 ch, miss 1 tr, 1 dbl tr into each of next
2 tr, 2 ch, 4 trip tr clusters with 4 ch between
each into next 4 ch loop; repeat from last *
ending with 2 ch, miss 1 tr, 1 dbl tr into each of
next 2 tr 2 ch, 1 dbl tr into 3rd of 5 ch, 5 ch,
turn.
6th row: Leaving the last loop of each on
hook work 1 tr into each of next 2 sps, thread
over and draw through all loops on hook (a
joint tr made), * 2 ch, 1 tr 3 ch and 1 tr into
each of next 3 sps, 2 ch, a joint tr over next 2
sps; repeat from * to corner, 2 ch, 1 tr 3 ch and
1 tr into each of next 2 sps, 1 tr 3 ch and 1 tr
into top of next cluster, 1 tr 3 ch and 1 tr into
each of next 2 sps, 2 ch, a joint tr over next 2
sps, * 2 ch, 1 tr 3 ch and 1 tr into each of next 3
sps, 2 ch, a joint tr over next 2 sps; repeat from
last * ending with 2 ch, 1 tr into 3rd of 6 ch,
1 ch, turn.
7th row: 1 dc into first tr, * 2 dc into each of
next 2 sps, (2 dc into next sp, 4 ch, 1 dc into top
of last dc, 2 dc into same sp) 3 times; repeat
from * to corner, 2 dc into each of next 2 sps, (2
dc into next sp, 4 ch, 1 dc into top of last dc, 2
dc into same sp) 5 times, * 2 dc into each of
next 2 sps, (2 dc into next sp, 4 ch, 1 dc into top
of last dc, 2 dc into same sp) 3 times; repeat
from last * ending with 2 dc into each of next 2
sps, 1 dc into 3rd of 5 ch. Fasten off.
Work another edging to correspond for other
curtain.
Slipstitch edgings in place on cotton.
Damp and press.

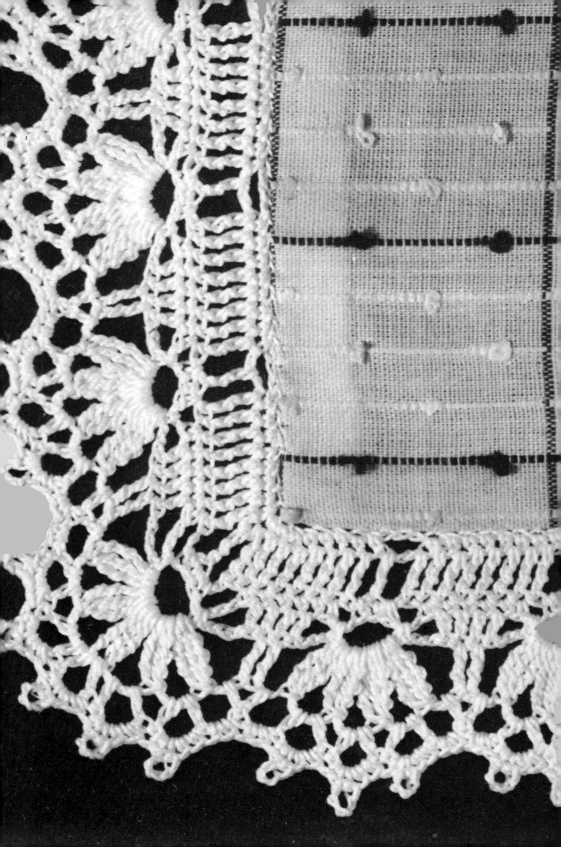

Lunch set

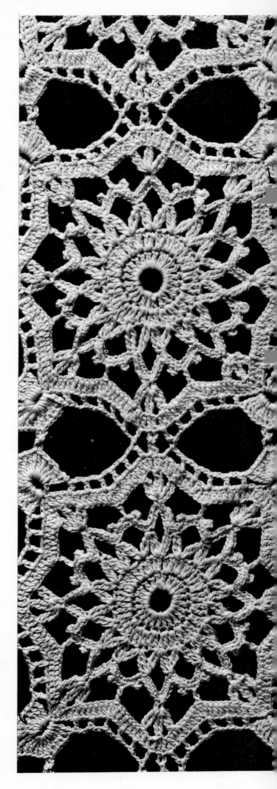

Materials: Coats Mercer-Crochet no. 40
(20 grms).
5 balls.
This model is worked in shade 962 (Dk Buttercup), but any other shade of Mercer-Crochet
may be used.
Milward steel crochet hook 1·00 (no. 4), or size
to fit tension (gauge).
10 motifs and 4 fillings may be worked from 1
ball.
Size of motif: $3\frac{1}{4}$ ins (8·1 cms) diameter.

Measurements: Centrepiece: $9\frac{3}{4} \times 16\frac{1}{2}$ ins.
(24·8 × 41 cms).
Place Mat: $9\frac{3}{4} \times 13$ ins (24·8 × 33 cms).

Centrepiece

First motif

Commence with 11 ch, join with a ss to form
a ring.
1st row: 3 ch, 23 tr into ring, 1 ss into 3rd of
3 ch.
2nd row: 3 ch, 1 tr into same place as ss, 2 tr
into each tr, 1 ss into 3rd of 3 ch.
3rd row: 4 ch, 1 dbl tr into same place as ss,
* 9 ch, leaving the last loop of each on hook
work 2 dbl tr into same place as last dbl tr
miss 2 tr and 2 dbl tr into next tr, thread over
and draw through all loops on hook; repeat
from * ending with 9 ch, leaving the last loop
of each on hook work 2 dbl tr into same place
as last dbl tr, thread over and draw through
all loops on hook (a 2 dbl tr cluster made), 1 ss
into first dbl tr.
4th row: * 1 dc into each of next 5 ch, 5 ch,
1 ss into last dc, 1 dc into each of next 7 ch,
4 ch, 1 ss into last dc (a picot made), 1 dc into
each of next 4 ch, a picot, 1 dc into each of
next 2 ch; repeat from * ending with 1 ss into
first dc.

5th row: 1 ss into each of first 4 dc and into 5 ch loop, 4 ch, 1 dbl tr into same loop, * (3 ch, a 2 dbl tr cluster into same loop) twice, 6 ch, miss next picot and 1 dc, 1 tr into next dc, 6 ch, a 2 dbl tr cluster into next 5 ch loop; repeat from * omitting a 2 dbl tr cluster at end of last repeat, 1 ss into first dbl tr.

6th row: 3 ch, * 1 tr into each of next 4 sts, 5 ch, 1 ss into last tr (a 5 ch loop made), 1 tr into each of next 9 sts, leaving the last loop of each on hook work 1 tr into each of next 3 sts, thread over and draw through all loops on hook (a cluster made over 3 sts), 1 tr into each of next 10 sts, 9 ch, 1 ss into last tr (a 9 ch loop made), 1 tr into each of next 9 sts, a cluster over next 3 sts, 1 tr into each of next 6 sts; repeat from * omitting 1 tr at end of last repeat, 1 ss into 3rd of 3 ch. Fasten off.

Second motif

Work as first motif for 5 rows.

6th row: 3 ch, 1 tr into each of next 4 sts, 2 ch, 1 ss into any 5 ch loop on first motif, 2 ch, 1 ss into last tr on second motif, 1 tr into each of next 9 sts and complete to correspond with first motif. Make 3 rows of 5 motifs joining each as second motif was joined to first.

Filling

With right side facing attach thread to any free 9 ch loop between joinings, 4 ch, into same loop work 5 dbl tr 5 ch 1 ss into last dbl tr (another 5 ch loop made) 5 dbl tr 7 ch 1 ss into last dbl tr (a 7 ch loop made) 5 dbl tr a 5 ch loop and 6 dbl tr, * miss 3 tr on motif, 1 tr into next st, (2 ch, miss 2 sts, 1 tr into next st) 5 times, miss 1 tr after join on next motif, 1 tr into next st, (2 ch, miss 2 sts, 1 tr into next st) 5 times, 6 dbl tr into next 9 ch loop, 2 ch, remove loop from hook, insert hook into last 5 ch loop made and draw dropped loop through, 3 ch, 1 ss into last dbl tr (a joining 5 ch loop made), 5 dbl tr into same 9 ch loop, 3 ch, remove loop from hook, insert hook into first 7 ch loop made and draw dropped loop through, 4 ch, 1 ss into last dbl tr, (a joining 7 ch loop made), into same 9 ch loop work 5 dbl tr a 5 ch loop and 6 dbl tr; repeat from * twice more omitting a 5 ch loop and 6 dbl tr at end of last repeat, 2 ch, remove loop from hook, insert hook into first 5 ch loop made and draw dropped loop through, 3 ch, 1 ss into last dbl tr, 6 dbl tr into same 9 ch loop, miss 3 tr on motif, 1 tr into next st, (2 ch, miss 2 sts, 1 tr into next st) 5 times, miss 1 tr after join on next motif, 1 tr into next st, (2 ch, miss 2 sts, 1 tr into next st) 5 times, 1 ss into 4th of 4 ch. Fasten off. Fill in all sps between motifs in this manner.

Edging

With right side facing attach thread to 9 ch loop at any corner, 4 ch, into same loop work 5 dbl tr a 5 ch loop 5 dbl tr a 7 ch loop 5 dbl tr 5 ch loop and 6 dbl tr, * * miss 3 tr on motif, 1 tr into next st, (2 ch, miss 2 sts, 1 tr into next st) 5 times, 2 ch, into next 5 ch loop work 1 tr 2 ch 1 tr a 5 ch loop 2 ch and 1 tr, 2 ch, miss 1 tr on motif, 1 tr into next st, (2 ch, miss 2 sts, 1 tr into next st) 5 times, * into next 9 ch loop work 6 dbl tr a 5 ch loop 5 dbl tr a 7 ch loop 5 dbl tr 5 ch loop and 6 dbl tr (a shell made), miss 3 tr on motif, 1 tr into next st, (2 ch, miss 2 sts, 1 tr into next st) 5 times, miss 1 tr after join on next motif, 1 tr into next st, (2 ch, miss 2 sts, 1 tr into next st) 5 times, into next 9 ch loop work 6 dbl tr a joining 5 ch loop 5 dbl tr a joining 7 ch loop 5 dbl tr a 5 ch loop and 6 dbl tr, miss 3 tr on motif, 1 tr into next st, (2 ch, miss 2 sts, 1 tr into next st) 5 times, 2 ch, into next 5 ch loop work 1 tr 2 ch 1 tr a 5 ch loop 2 ch and 1 tr, 2 ch, miss 1 tr on motif, 1 tr into next st, (2 ch, miss 2 sts, 1 tr into next st) 5 times; repeat from * to within next corner 9 ch loop, a shell into 9 ch loop; repeat from * * omitting a shell at end of last repeat, 1 ss into 4th of 4 ch. Fasten off.

Place mat (make 2)

Make 3 rows of 4 motifs joining as before. Work filling and edging as Centrepiece. Damp and pin out to measurements.

Lampshade trimming

Materials: Coats Mercer-Crochet no. 10
(20 grms).
2 balls.
This model is worked in shade 524 (Dk Jade),
but any other shade of Mercer-Crochet may be
used.
Milward steel crochet hook 1·50 (no. 2½).

Tension (gauge): 10 dc: 1 in.

Measurements: Top edging: ⅝ × 26 ins,
adjustable. Lower edging: 1¼ × 32¼ ins, adjustable.

Top edging

Commence with a length of chain to measure
26 ins or length required having 10 ch to 1 in
and a multiple of 3 ch, being careful not to
twist join with a ss to form a ring.
1st row: 1 dc into same place as ss, 1 dc into
each ch, 1 ss into first dc.
2nd row: 1 dc into each dc, 1 ss into first dc.
3rd row: 5 ch, * miss 2 dc, 1 tr into next dc,
2 ch; repeat from * ending with 1 ss into 3rd of
5 ch.
4th row: 1 dc into same place as ss, * 2 dc into
next sp, 1 dc into next tr; repeat from *
omitting 1 dc at end of last repeat, 1 ss into
first dc.
5th row: As 2nd row. Fasten off.

Lower edging

Commence with 8 ch.
1st row: 1 tr into 8th ch from hook, 5 ch, turn.
2nd row: Miss 2 ch, 1 tr into next ch, 5 ch,
turn.
Repeat last row until work measures 32 ins or
length required having a multiple 3 sps and
omitting turning ch at end of last row. Fasten
off.
Place last row to foundation ch and sew
neatly.

Heading

1st row: Attach thread to sp at left of join, 3
dc into same sp, 3 dc into each sp, 1 ss into first
dc.
2nd row: 1 dc into each dc, 1 ss into first dc.
Fasten off.

Edging

1st row: Attach thread to opposite side of sps
and work as first row of heading.
2nd row: 1 ss into next dc, 1 dc into same
place as ss, * 1 dc into each of next 8 dc, 12 ch,
remove hook, insert hook into last dc and
draw loop through, into loop just formed work
1 dc, remove hook insert hook into 3rd last dc
and draw loop through 1 hlf tr 18 tr 1 hlf tr and
1 dc, 1 ss into next dc on previous row, 1 dc
into same place as ss; repeat from * omitting
1 ss and 1 dc at end of last repeat, 1 ss into first
dc. Fasten off.
Damp and pin out to measurements.

To make up

Place crochet round top and lower edges of
lampshade as shown in illustration. Sew
neatly in position.

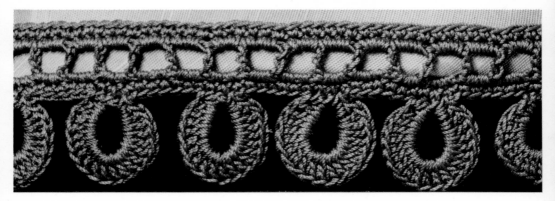

Guest towel edging

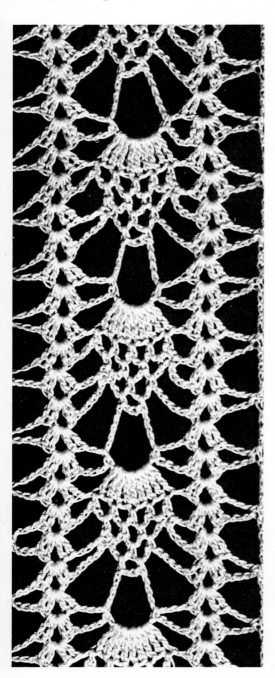

Materials: Coats Mercer-Crochet no. 20 (20 grms).
1 ball.
This model was worked in White but any desired colour may be used.
1 towel.
Milward steel crochet hook 1·25 (no. 3), or size to fit tension (gauge).

Depth of edging: 2 ins.

Commence with 20 ch.
1st row: 2 tr 2 ch and 2 tr into 8th ch from hook (shell made), 7 ch, miss next 4 ch, 1 dc into next ch, 3 ch, miss 1 ch, 1 dc into next ch, 7 ch, miss 4 ch, 2 tr 2 ch and 2 tr into next ch (another shell made), 7 ch, turn.
2nd row: Shell into sp of shell (shell made over shell), 4 ch, 1 dc into next loop, 5 ch, miss next 3 ch loop, 1 dc into next loop, 4 ch, shell over shell, 7 ch, turn.
3rd row: Shell over shell, 1 ch, miss next loop, 9 dbl tr into next loop, 1 ch, shell over shell, 7 ch, turn.
4th row: Shell over shell, 3 ch, 1 dc into next dbl tr, (3 ch, miss next dbl tr, 1 dc into next dbl tr), 4 times, 3 ch, shell over shell, 7 ch, turn.
5th row: Shell over shell, 4 ch, miss next sp, (1 dc into next loop, 3 ch) 3 times, 1 dc into each of next 2 loops, 4 ch, shell over shell, 7 ch, turn.
6th row: Shell over shell, 5 ch, miss next sp, (1 dc into next loop, 3 ch) twice, 1 dc into each of next 2 loops, 5 ch, shell over shell, 7 ch, turn.
7th row: Shell over shell, 7 ch, miss next sp, 1 dc into next loop, 3 ch, 1 dc into next loop, 7 ch, shell over shell, 7 ch, turn. Repeat 2nd to 7th row until piece is length required, ending on a 7th row of pattern.
Next row: Shell over shell, 5 ch, miss next sp, 1 dbl tr into next loop, 5 ch, shell over shell. Fasten off.

Heading
Attach thread to last 7 ch loop on long side, 1 dc into same loop, * 5 ch, 1 dc into next loop; repeat from * across.
Fasten off. Starch lightly and press. Sew neatly to towel.

Trolley cloth

Materials: Coats Mercer-Crochet no. 20
(20 grms).
4 balls.
This model is worked in shade 510 (Cobalt
Blue), but any other shade of Mercer-Crochet
may be used.
Milward steel crochet hook 1·25 (no. 3) or size
to fit tension (gauge).
6 motifs and 2 fillings may be worked from 1
ball.

Tension (gauge): Size of motif: 4 ins (10 cms)
diameter.
Measurements: 16× 20 ins (40·5× 50·5 cms).

First motif

Commence with 10 ch, join with a ss to form a
ring.
1st row: 3 ch, 23 tr into ring, 1 ss into 3rd of
3 ch.
2nd row: 10 ch, thread over hook twice, insert
hook into 8th ch from hook and draw thread
through, thread over hook, miss 1 tr, insert
hook into next tr and draw thread through,
(thread over hook and draw through 2 loops)
5 times, * 3 ch, thread over hook 4 times, insert
hook into next tr and draw thread through,
(thread over and draw through 2 loops) twice,
thread over hook, miss 1 tr, insert hook into
next tr and draw thread through, (thread over
hook and draw through 2 loops) 5 times, 3 ch,
1 tr into centre point of cross (cross completed); repeat from * ending with 3 ch, 1 ss
into 7th of 10 ch.
3rd row: 5 dc into each sp.
4th to 7th row: 1 dc into each dc ending last
row with 1 ss into first dc.
8th row: 4 ch, 1 tr into next dc, * 1 ch, 1 tr into
next dc; repeat from * ending with 1 ch, 1 ss
into 3rd·of 4 ch.

9th row: 1 ss into next ch, 10 ch, thread over
hook twice, insert hook into 8th ch from hook
and draw thread through, thread over hook,
miss next sp, insert hook into next sp and
draw thread through, (thread over and draw
through 2 loops) 5 times, * 3 ch, thread over
hook 4 times, miss next sp, insert hook into
next sp and draw thread through, (thread over
and draw through 2 loops) twice, thread over
hook, miss next sp, insert hook into next sp
and draw thread through, (thread over and
draw through 2 loops) 5 times, 3 ch, 1 tr into
centre point of cross; repeat from * ending
with 3 ch, 1 ss into 7th of 10 ch.
10th row: 1 ss into next ch and into same sp,
5 ch, 1 tr into same sp, * 3 ch, 1 dc into next sp,
3 ch, into next sp work 1 tr 2 ch and 1 tr;
repeat from * omitting 1 tr 2 ch and 1 tr at end
of last repeat, 1 ss into 3rd of 5 ch.
11th row: 1 ss into first sp, 6 ch, 1 tr into same
sp, * 4 ch, 1 dc into next dc, 4 ch, into next 2 ch
sp work 1 tr 3 ch and 1 tr; repeat from * omitting 1 tr 3 ch and 1 tr at end of last repeat, 1 ss
into 3rd of 6 ch. Fasten off.

Second motif

Work as first motif for 10 rows.
11th row: 1 ss into first sp, 6 ch, 1 tr into same
sp, (4 ch, 1 dc into next dc, 4 ch, 1 tr into next
2 ch sp, 1 ch, 1 dc into corresponding sp on
first motif, 1 ch, 1 tr into same sp on second
motif) 3 times, 4 ch, 1 dc into next dc and complete as first motif.
Make 4 rows of 5 motifs joining each as second
motif was joined to first and leaving two
points free between joinings.

Filling

Commence with 4 ch, join with a ss to form a
ring.
1st row: * 15 ch, 1 dc into join, 15 ch, 1 dc into
ring, (9 ch, 1 dc into next free point, 9 ch, 1 dc
into ring) twice; repeat from * 3 times more.
Fasten off. Fill in all spaces in this manner.
Damp and pin out to measurements.

Fashion crochet

Long evening skirt

Materials: Of Double Knitting yarn, 14/15/16/17 (20 grms) balls in Dark Shade and 11/12/13/14 (20 grms) balls in Light Shade.
No. 9 (3·50 mm) crochet hook, or size to fit tension (gauge).
8 ins zip.
Length of 1½ ins wide petersham or stiff ribbon and 2 hooks and eyes for waistband.
8 yds each ⅞ in wide ribbon in 4 contrasting shades.

Measurements: To fit 34/36/38/40 ins hips; length, 38½ ins all sizes.

Tension: 20 sts and 9 rows measured over 4 ins of pattern.

Abbreviations: l tr=long treble worked as follows: (yarn round hook) 4 times, insert hook in next st and draw loop through, (yrh, draw through 2 loops) 4 times. Decr 1=yarn round hook, draw loop through each of next 2 sts, yrh, draw loop through all 4 loops on hook.
D=1st Contrast. L=2nd Contrast.

Back and front alike
With D, make 116/121/126/131 ch.
Foundation row: 1 hlf tr in 3rd ch from hook, 1 hlf tr in each ch to end: 115/120/125/130 sts.
Continue in pattern as follows:
1st row: 5 ch, miss 1st st, 1 l tr in each st ending with 1 l tr in 2nd of 2 ch.
2nd row: 2 ch, miss 1st st, 1 hlf tr in each st ending with 1 hlf tr in 5th of 5 ch.
3rd row: 2 ch, miss 1st st, l tr in next st, * 3 ch, miss 1st, l tr in each of next 4 sts; rep from * to last 3 sts, 3 ch, miss 1 st, l tr in next st, l tr in 2nd of 2 ch.
4th row: 4 ch, * 1 dc in ch sp, 2 ch, miss 1 tr, 1 tr in each of next 2 tr, 2 ch, miss 1 tr; rep

from * ending with 1 dc in last ch sp, 2 ch, 1 tr in 2nd of 2 ch.
5th row: 2 ch, 1 tr in 2 ch sp, * 1 ch, 1 tr in 2 ch sp, 1 tr in each of next 2 tr, 1 tr in 2 ch sp; rep from * ending with 1 ch, 1 tr in last 2 ch sp, 1 tr in 2nd of 4 ch.
6th row: 2 ch, 1 hlf tr in 1 tr, * 1 hlf tr in ch sp, 1 hlf tr in each of next 4 tr; rep from * ending with 1 hlf tr in last ch sp, 1 hlf tr in last tr, 1 hlf tr in 2nd of 2 ch.
7th and 8th rows: As 1st and 2nd.
Break D. Join in L.
9th row: In L, as 2nd.
10th–17th rows: In L, as 1st–8th rows.
Break L. Rejoin D.
18th row: In D, as 2nd.
These 18 rows form pattern.
Work a further 19 rows straight, thus ending with 1st pattern row. Continue in pattern, shaping skirt as follows: †
1st decrease row: 2 ch, 1 hlf tr in each of next 9/10/10/11 sts, (Decr 1, 1 hlf tr in each of next 21/22/23/24 sts) 4 times, Decr 1, 1 hlf tr in each of last 10/10/11/11 sts, 1 hlf tr in 5th of 5 ch: 110/115/120/125 sts. Work 5 rows straight in pattern.
2nd decrease row: 2 ch, 1 hlf tr in each of next 9/9/10/10 sts, (Decr 1, 1 hlf tr in each of next 20/21/22/23 sts) 4 times, Decr 1, 1 hlf tr in each of last 9/10/10/11 sts, 1 hlf tr in 5th of 5 ch: 105/110/115/120 sts. Work 2 rows straight.
3rd decrease row: 2 ch, 1 hlf tr in each of next 8/9/9/10 sts, (Decr 1, 1 hlf tr in each of next 19/20/21/22 sts) 4 times, Decr 1, 1 hlf tr in each of last 9/9/10/10 sts, 1 hlf tr in 5th of 5 ch: 100/105/110/115 sts. Work 5 rows straight.
4th decrease row: 2 ch, 1 hlf tr in each of next 8/8/9/9 sts, (Decr 1, 1 hlf tr in each of next 18/19/20/21 sts) 4 times, Decr 1, 1 hlf tr in each of last 8/9/9/10 sts, 1 hlf tr in 5th of 5 ch: 95/100/105/110 sts. Work 2 rows straight.

5th decrease row: 2 ch. 1 hlf tr in each of
next 7/8/8/9 sts, (Decr 1, 1 hlf tr in each of
next 17/18/19/20 sts) 4 times, Decr 1, 1 hlf tr in each
of last 8/8/9/9 sts, 1 hlf tr in 5th of 5 ch:
90/95/100/105 sts. Work 5 rows straight.

6th decrease row: 2 ch, 1 hlf tr in each of
next 7/7/8/8 sts, (Decr 1, 1 hlf tr in each of next
16/17/18/19 sts) 4 times, Decr 1, 1 hlf tr in each
of last 7/8/8/9 sts, 1 hlf tr in 5th of 5 ch: 85/90/
95/100 sts. Work 2 rows straight.

7th decrease row: 2 ch, 1 hlf tr in each of
next 6/7/7/8 sts, (Decr 1, 1 hlf tr in each of next
15/16/17/18 sts) 4 times, Decr 1, 1 hlf tr in each
of last 7/7/8/8 sts, 1 hlf tr in 5th of 5 ch:
80/85/90/95 sts. Work 5 rows straight.

8th decrease row: 2 ch, 1 hlf tr, in each of
next 6/6/7/7 sts, (Decr 1, 1 hlf tr in each of next
14/15/16/17 sts) 4 times, Decr 1, 1 hlf tr in each
of last 6/7/7/8 sts, 1 hlf tr in 5th of 5 ch:
75/80/85/90 sts. Work 2 rows straight.

9th decrease row: 2 ch, 1 hlf tr in each of
next 5/6/6/7 sts, (Decr 1, 1 hlf tr in each of next
13/14/15/16 sts) 4 times, Decr 1, 1 hlf tr in each
of last 6/6/7/7 sts, 1 hlf tr in 5th of 5 ch:
70/75/80/85 sts. Work 5 rows straight.

10th decrease row: 2 ch, 1 hlf tr in each of
next 5/5/6/6 sts, (Decr 1, 1 hlf tr in each of next
12/13/14/15 sts) 4 times, Decr 1, 1 hlf tr in each
of last 5/6/6/7 sts, 1 hlf tr in 5th of 5 ch:
65/70/75/80 sts.

Continue in hlf tr in D, and work a further 5
rows straight for waistband. Fasten off.

To make up

Using a warm iron and damp cloth, press parts
lightly on wrong side. Join right side seam,
then join left side seam leaving 8 ins open for
zip.

Thread ribbon loosely through each 1 tr row,
alternating colours as illustrated. Cut
petersham to fit waist and sew inside waistband. Sew on hooks and eyes. Press seams.

Picot border

With right side facing and D, work all round
lower edge as follows: * 2 ch, 1 dc in 2nd ch
from hook, miss 1 st, ss in next st; rep from *
all round. Fasten off. Press border lightly.

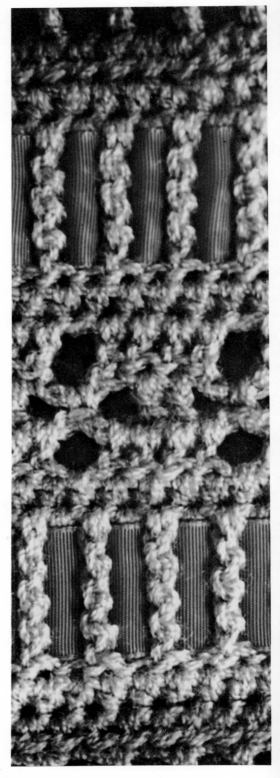

Hat, scarf and bag

Materials: Of Double Knitting yarn,
Hat: 1 (1 oz) ball each in Rust, in Camel, in
Black and in White.
Scarf: 2 (1 oz) balls each in Rust, in Camel, in
Black and in White.
Bag: 2 (1 oz) balls each in Rust and in Black
and 1 (1 oz) ball each in Camel and in White.
No. 8 (4 mms) and no. 9 (3·50 mms) crochet
hooks. 1¾ yds, 1½ ins wide petersham or stiff
ribbon and ½ yd lining for bag.

Measurements:
Hat: Average hat size.
Scarf: Width, 6 ins; length, 68 ins (excluding
fringes).
Bag: 10½ ins diameter.

Abbreviations:
R = Rust, C = Camel, W=White, B=Black.

Hat

* * With no. 8 hook and R, make 5 ch. Join
with ss to form a ring.
1st round: 2 ch, 11 tr into ring: 12 sts. Join
with ss in 2nd of 2 ch.
2nd round: In R, 2 ch, * 2 tr in next st; rep
from * ending with 1 tr in base of 2 ch; 24 sts.
Join with ss.
Join in B.
3rd round: In B, 2 ch, * 2 hlf tr in next
st, 1 hlf tr in next st; rep from * ending with 2
hlf tr in last st: 36 sts. Join with ss. Join in W.
4th round: In W, 2 ch, 1 hlf tr in each st all
round. Join with ss. Join in C.
5th round: In C, 2 ch, * 2 tr in next st, 1 tr in
each of next 2 sts; rep from * ending with 1 tr
in last st: 48 sts. Join with ss.
6th round: In C, 2 ch, * 2 tr in next st, 1 tr in
each of next 3 sts; rep from * ending with 1 tr
in each of last 2 sts: 60 sts. Join with ss.
Note: Carry yarns loosely up back of work.

7th round: In W, 2 ch, * 2 hlf tr in next st, 1
hlf tr in each of next 4 sts; rep from * ending
with 1 hlf tr in each of last 3 sts: 72 sts. Join
with ss.
8th round: In B, as 4th * *.
9th round: In R, 2 ch, * 1 tr in each st all
round. Join with ss.
10th round: In R, 2 ch, * 2 tr in next st, 1 tr
in each of next 5 sts; rep from * ending with 1
tr in each of last 4 sts: 84 sts. Join with ss.
11th round: As 8th.
12th round: As 4th.

13th round: In C, 2 ch, 2 tr in next st, 1 tr in each of next 6 sts; rep from * ending with 1 tr in each of last 5 sts: 96 sts. Join with ss.
14th round: In C, as 9th.
15th round: As 4th.
16th round: As 8th.
17th and 18th rounds: As 9th.
19th round: As 8th.
20th round: As 4th.
21st round: As 14th.
Change to no. 9 hook.
22nd round: As 14th.
23rd round: As 4th.
24th round: As 8th, but turning work and working with wrong side facing all round. Join with ss. Fasten off.

Scarf

With no. 8 hook and B, make 301 ch.
Foundation row: In B, 1 hlf tr in 3rd ch from hook, 1 hlf tr in each ch to end: 300 sts. Join in W and pattern as follows:
1st row: In W, 2 ch, miss 1st st, 1 hlf tr in each st, ending with 1 hlf tr in 2nd of 2 ch. Join in C.
2nd and 3rd rows: In C, 2 ch, miss 1st st, 1 tr in each st, ending with 1 tr in 2nd of 2 ch.
4th row: As 1st.
5th row: In B, as 1st. Join in R.
6th and 7th rows: In R, as 2nd and 3rd.
8th row: As 5th. These 8 rows form pattern.
Note: Carry yarns loosely up sides of work.
Repeat rows 1–8 inclusive, then 1st row again. Fasten off.

Bag

Work as for hat from * * to * *.
9th round: In R, 2 ch, * 2 tr in next st, 1 tr in each of next 5 sts; rep from * ending with 1 tr in each of last 4 sts: 84 sts. Join with ss.
10th round: In R, 2 ch, * 2 tr in next st, 1 tr in each of next 6 sts; rep from * ending with 1 tr in each of last 5 sts: 96 sts. Join with ss.
11th round: In B, 2 ch, * 2 hlf tr in next st, 1 hlf tr in each of next 7 sts; rep from * ending with 1 hlf tr in each of last 6 sts: 108 sts. Join with ss.
12th round: In W, 2 ch, 1 hlf tr in each st all round.
13th round: In C, 2 ch, * 2 tr in next st, 1 tr in each of next 8 sts; rep from * ending with 1 tr in each of last 7 sts: 120 sts. Join with ss.
14th round: In C, 2 ch, * 2 tr in next st, 1 tr in each of next 9 sts; rep from * ending with 1 tr in each of last 8 sts. Join with ss: 132 sts.

15th round: In W, 2 ch, * 2 hlf tr in next st, 1 hlf tr in each of next 10 sts; rep from * ending with 1 hlf tr in each of last 9 sts: 144 sts. Join with ss.
16th round: In B, as 12th. Fasten off. Make another circle the same.

Handle: With B, make 261 ch.
Foundation row: 1 hlf tr in 3rd ch from hook, 1 hlf tr in each ch to end: 260 sts. Break B. Join in R.
Next row: In R, 2 ch, miss 1st st, 1 tr in each st ending with 1 tr in 2nd of 2 ch. Rep last row twice more. Break R.
Rejoin B.
Next row: 2 ch, miss 1st st, 1 hlf tr in each st ending with 1 hlf tr in 2nd of 2 ch. Fasten off.

To make up

Using a warm iron and damp cloth, press parts lightly on wrong side. Darn in short ends of yarn on wrong side.

Scarf

Cut remaining yarn into 12 ins lengths. Using 6 strands together each time, double yarn and knot into short ends of scarf, alternating colours as illustrated. Trim fringes.

Bag

Cut 2 circles of cardboard 10 ins in diameter, then cut 2 circles of lining, each 11 ins in diameter.
Place a cardboard circle in centre of each lining circle and glue ½ in turnings of lining on to card, clipping at intervals to make a neat fold all round.
Sew lining and card circle to crochet circle, wrong sides together, catching edge of lining circle ¼ in away from outer edge of crochet circle.
Join short ends of handle together. Cut petersham 1 in longer than handle. Join short ends together ½ in away from end. Press join open. Pin petersham in centre of handle, wrong sides together and sew in position all round.
Pin join on handle at point on circle where work was fastened off. Count 48 sts on circle and handle from this point in each direction and mark with pins.
Using no. 9 hook and B and with right side of handle facing, crochet bag and handle together in dc between the 2 marked points. Fasten off and work other side to correspond.

Snood

Materials: Coats Mercer-Crochet no. 20
(20 grms).
2 balls.
This model is worked in White, but any shade
of Mercer-Crochet may be used.
Milward steel crochet hook 1·25 (no. 3), or size
to fit tension (gauge).
Shirring elastic.

Tension (gauge):
First 2 rows – 1¼ ins diameter.
　　Flower – 1¾ ins diameter.

Measurements: Centre of crown to finished
edge 10 ins.

Note: *Snood may be pinned out to shape before
band is worked or, if preferred, may be
stretched over hat block on completion of band.*

Crown
Commence with 2 ch.
1st row: 8 dc into 2nd ch from hook, 1 ss into
first dc.
2nd row: 1 dc into same place as ss, * draw
loop on hook out ⅜ in, thread over hook and
draw through loop on hook, insert hook
between loop and single thread of this ch and
make a dc (knot st made), 1 knot st (solomon's
knot made), 1 dc into next dc; repeat from *
working last dc into first dc, 1 solomon's knot,
1 dc into dc at centre of first solomon's knot.
3rd row: * 1 solomon's knot, 1 knot st
(increase loop made), 1 dc into centre dc of
next solomon's knot; repeat from * working
last dc into first dc of first increase loop.
4th row: * 1 solomon's knot, 1 dc into next dc
of same increase loop, 1 solomon's knot, 1 dc
into first dc of next increase loop; repeat from
* working last dc into centre dc of first solomon's knot.
5th and 6th rows: * 1 solomon's knot, 1 dc
into centre dc of next solomon's knot; repeat

from * ending with 1 solomon's knot, 1 dc into
centre dc of first solomon's knot.
7th row: As 3rd row.
8th row: As 4th row. (35 solomon's knots).
9th to 13th row: As 5th row.
14th row: * (1 solomon's knot, 1 dc into centre
dc of next solomon's knot) 4 times, 1 increase
loop, 1 dc into centre of next solomon's knot;
repeat from * ending with 1 solomon's knot, 1
dc into centre dc of first solomon's knot.
15th row: * (1 solomon's knot, 1 dc into centre
dc of next solomon's knot) 3 times, 1 solomon's
knot, 1 dc into first dc of next increase loop, 1
solomon's knot, 1 dc into next dc of same
increase loop, 1 solomon's knot, 1 dc into
centre dc of next solomon's knot; repeat from
* ending with 1 solomon's knot, 1 dc into centre dc of first solomon's knot. (42 solomon's
knots).
16th row: As 5th row.
17th row: As 14th row ending with (1 solomon's knot, 1 dc into centre dc of next solomon's knot) twice, 1 solomon's knot, 1 dc into
centre dc of first solomon's knot.
18th row: As 15th row ending with (1 solomon's knot, 1 dc into centre dc of next
solomon's knot) twice, 1 solomon's knot, 1 dc
into centre dc of first solomon's knot.
19th to 24th row: As 5th row. Do not fasten
off.

Band
1st row: * (4 ch, 1 dc into centre dc of next
solomon's knot) twice, 5 ch, 1 dc into centre dc
of next solomon's knot; repeat from * ending
with 1 dc into last dc of previous row.
2nd row: 1 ss into next sp, 3 ch, 4 tr into same
sp, 5 tr into each sp, 1 ss into 3rd of 3 ch.
3rd to 6th row: 3 ch, 1 tr into each tr, 1 ss into
3rd of 3 ch.
7th row: Working over shirring elastic used
double, 1 dc into same place as ss, 1 dc into
each tr, 1 ss into first dc. Fasten off.

Flower *make 6*
Commence with 4 ch, join with a ss to form a
ring.
1st row: (1 dc into ring, 10 ch, 1 dc into 3rd ch
from hook, 1 hlf tr into next ch 1 tr into next
ch, 1 dbl tr into each of next 2 ch, 1 tr into next
ch, 1 hlf tr into next ch, 1 dc into next ch)
6 times, 1 ss into first dc. Fasten off.
Damp and pin out to measurements.
Sew flowers to band *(see illustration).*

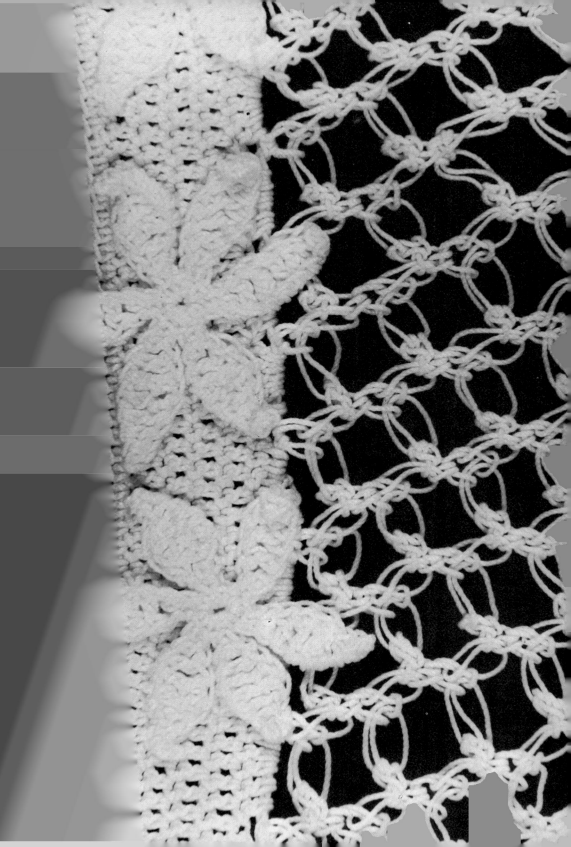

Beret

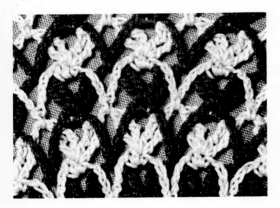

Materials: Coats Mercer-Crochet no. 20 (20 grms).
3 balls 579 (Brown) and 2 balls 680 (Pale Glacier Blue).
This model is worked in the two shades but any other shades of Mercer-Crochet may be used.
Milward steel crochet hook 1·25 (no. 3), or size to fit tension (gauge).
1 yd fabric 36 ins wide for lining.
3 yds tubular elastic.

Tension: First 2 rows = ¾ in diameter.

Measurements: Diameter across crown = 11½ ins approximately.

It is advisable when working this design to weave thread not in use across row ends.
Using Blue commence with 6 ch, join with a ss to form a ring.
1st row: 12 dc into ring, 1 ss into first dc.
2nd row: 3 ch, 1 tr into same place as ss, 2 tr into each dc, 1 ss into 3rd of 3 ch.
3rd row: 1 dc into same place as ss, * 2 ch, 1 dc into next tr; repeat from * ending with 2 ch,

1 ss into first dc.
4th row: 1 ss into next loop, 4 ch, into same loop work 1 dbl tr 2 ch and 2 dbl tr, * 1 ch, miss next loop, into next loop work 2 dbl tr 2 ch and 2 dbl tr (a shell made); repeat from * ending with 1 ch, miss next loop, 1 ss into 4th of 4 ch.
5th row: 1 ss into next dbl tr, drop Blue, attach Brown, 1 ss into next sp, 3 dc into same sp, * 4 ch, keeping hook to front of work, 1 dc into next free loop on 3rd row, 4 ch, 3 dc into sp of next shell; repeat from * omitting 3 dc at end of last repeat, 1 ss into first dc.
6th row: 1 ss into next dc, 4 ch, into same place work 1 dbl tr 2 ch and 2 dbl tr, * 1 ch, a shell into centre dc of next group, 3 ch, a shell into centre dc of next group; repeat from * omitting a shell at end of last repeat, 1 ss into 4th of 4 ch.
7th row: 1 ss into next dbl tr, drop Brown, pick up Blue, 1 ss into next sp, 3 dc into same sp, * 4 ch, keeping hook to front of work, 1 dc into next 1 ch sp on 4th row, 4 ch, 3 dc into sp of next shell; repeat from * omitting 3 dc at end of last repeat, 1 ss into first dc.
8th row: 1 ss into next dc, 4 ch, into same place work 1 dbl tr 2 ch and 2 dbl tr, * 3 ch, a shell into centre dc of next group; repeat from * ending with 3 ch, 1 ss into 4th of 4 ch.
9th row: 1 ss into next dbl tr, drop Blue, pick up Brown, 1 ss into next sp, 3 dc into same sp, * 5 ch, keeping hook to front of work, 1 dc into next sp on 6th row, 5 ch, 3 dc into sp of next shell; repeat from * omitting 3 dc at end of last repeat, 1 ss into first dc.
10th row: 1 dc into same place as ss, 1 dc into each of next 2 dc, * 5 ch, 1 hlf tr into centre ch of next sp on 8th row, 5 ch, 1 dc into each of next 3 dc; repeat from * omitting 3 dc at end of last repeat, 1 ss into first dc.
11th row: 3 ch, 1 tr into each st, 1 ss into 3rd of 3 ch. (168 sts).
12th and 13th rows: As 11th row.
14th row: 1 dc into same place as ss, * 2 ch, miss 1 tr, 1 dc into next tr; repeat from * omitting 1 dc at end of last repeat, 1 ss into first dc.
15th row: As 4th row, having 2 ch between shells.
16th row: 1 ss into next dbl tr, drop Brown, pick up Blue, 1 ss into next sp, 3 dc into same sp, * 4 ch, keeping hook to front of work, 1 dc into next sp on 14th row, 4 ch, 3 dc into sp of next shell; repeat from * omitting 3 dc at end of last repeat, 1 ss into first dc.

17th row: As 8th row, having 2 ch between shells.

18th row: 1 ss into next dbl tr, drop Blue, attach Brown, 1 ss into next sp, 3 dc into same sp, * 4 ch, keeping hook to front of work, 1 dc into next sp on 15th row, 4 ch, 3 dc into sp of next shell; repeat from * omitting 3 dc at end of last repeat, 1 ss into first dc.

19th row: As 8th row, having 2 ch between shells.

Last 4 rows from colour pattern.

Continue in this manner for 8 rows more.

28th row: 1 ss into next dbl tr, drop Brown, pick up Blue, 1 ss into next sp, 3 dc into same sp, * 5 ch, keeping hook to front of work, 1 dc into next sp on 25th row, 5 ch, 3 dc into sp of next shell; repeat from * omitting 3 dc at end of last repeat, 1 ss into first dc.

29th row: As 8th row.

30th row: 1 ss into next dbl tr, drop Blue, pick up Brown, 1 ss into next sp, 3 dc into same sp, * 5 ch, keeping hook to front of work, 1 dc into next sp on 27th row, 5 ch, 3 dc into sp of next shell; repeat from * omitting 3 dc at end of last repeat, 1 ss into first dc.

31st row: 1 dc into same place as ss, 1 dc into each of next 2 dc, * 3 ch, 1 hlf tr into centre ch of next sp on 29th row, 3 ch, 1 dc into each of next 3 dc; repeat from * omitting 3 dc at end of last repeat, 1 ss into first dc.

32nd row: 3 ch, 1 tr into each st, 1 ss into 3rd of 3 ch. (420 sts).

33rd to 36th row: As 32nd row.

37th row: 1 dc into same place as ss, * 3 ch, miss 2 tr, 1 dc into next tr; repeat from * omitting 1 dc at end of last repeat, 1 ss into first dc.

38th row: As 4th row.

39th row: As 16th row working into sp on 37th row.

40th row: As 8th row, having 1 ch between shells.

Keeping continuity of colour pattern, continue in this manner for 9 rows more.

50th row: 1 ss into next dc, 4 ch, into same place work 1 dbl tr 2 ch and 2 dbl tr, a shell into centre dc of each group, 1 ss into 4th of 4 ch.

51st row: 1 ss into next dbl tr and into next sp, 2 dc into same sp, * 2 ch, 2 dc into sp of next shell; repeat from * ending with 2 ch, 1 ss into first dc.

52nd row: 1 dc into same place as ss, 1 dc into next dc, * 2 dc into next sp, 1 dc into each of next 2 dc; repeat from * ending with 2 dc into last sp, 1 ss into first dc.

53rd to 57th row: 1 dc into each dc, 1 ss into first dc.

58th row: Working over elastic, 1 dc into each dc, 1 ss into first dc. Fasten off. Elastic may be adjusted to suit required head size.

Button

Using Blue, commence with 2 ch.

1st row: 6 dc into 2nd ch from hook.

2nd row: 2 dc into each dc.

3rd row: (1 dc into next dc, 2 dc into next dc) 6 times.

4th row: (1 dc into each of next 2 dc, 2 dc into next dc) 6 times.

5th row: (1 dc into each of next 3 dc, 2 dc into next dc) 6 times.

6th to 8th row: 1 dc into each dc.

9th row: * (Insert hook into next st and draw thread through) twice, thread over and draw through all loops on hook (a decrease made), 1 dc into each of next 3 dc; repeat from * 5 times more.

10th row: 1 dc into each dc.

11th row: * A dec over next 2 sts, 1 dc into each of next 2 dc; repeat from * 5 times more.

12th row: 1 dc into each dc. Fasten off leaving sufficient thread to lace through last row. Fill with cotton wool, draw up and secure. Sew on button.

Damp and pin out to measurements.

To make up

½ in seam allowance has been given.

Cut two circles of lining and one of interlining 12 ins in diameter for top and two crosswise strips of lining and one of interlining 4½ × 37 ins for side band.

Place interlining to wrong side of one lining section and baste. Stitch short ends of crosscut lining and interlining strips. Place interlining to wrong side of one lining strip and baste (this forms side band). Baste side band to outer edge of top, if necessary stretching slightly. Stitch in place. Stitch remaining lining sections in same manner. Place right sides of two completed sections together and stitch round outer edge leaving an opening sufficiently large to turn to the right side. Trim seams, turn to right side and slipstitch opening. Make 1 row of gathering stitches ¼ in from edge, draw up to size. Insert to wrong side of crochet and stitch in position.

Caps

for colour illustration, see page 69

Materials: Coats Mercer-Crochet no. 10
(20 grms).
3 balls 469 (Geranium) for man's cap.
3 balls 524 (Dk Jade) for lady's cap.
These models are worked in these two shades
but any other shades of Mercer-Crochet may
be used.
Coats 'Musica' health vest cotton, 2 oz ready-
wound balls. 2 balls for each cap.
Milward disc (aluminium) crochet hook 3·00
(no. 11), or size to fit tension (gauge).
¾ yd tubular elastic (sufficient for 2 caps).
¾ yd lining.
¾ yd interlining.

Tension (gauge): First 4 rows=2¼ ins.
Note: 6 dc=1 in measured over Mercer-
Crochet.
Note: 5 dc=1 in measured over health vest
cotton.

Measurements:
Diameter of top of crown – 9½ ins.
Circumference of last row – 22½ ins approxi-
mately.
Use Mercer-Crochet Double throughout.

Crown

Using Mercer-Crochet, commence with 6 ch,
join with a ss to form a ring.
1st row: 12 dc into ring, 1 ss into first dc.
2nd row: Attach health vest cotton and working over it 2 dc into each dc, drop Mercer-
Crochet, pick up health vest cotton, 1 ss into
first dc. Always change yarns in this manner.
3rd row: Working over Mercer-Crochet 1 dc
into each dc, 1 ss into first dc.
4th row: As 3rd row, change to Mercer-
Crochet.
5th row: Working over health vest cotton, 2

dc into each dc, 1 ss into first dc.
Always work over yarn not in use.
6th row: 2 dc into same place as ss, * 1 dc into
each of next 5 dc, 2 dc into next dc; repeat
from * omitting 2 dc at end of last repeat, 1 ss
into first dc. (56 dc).
7th row: 2 dc into same place as ss, * 1 dc into
each of next 6 dc, 2 dc into next dc; repeat
from * omitting 2 dc at end of last repeat, 1 ss
into first dc, change to health vest cotton.
(64 dc).
8th to 10th row: 1 dc into each dc, 1 ss in to
first dc.
11th row: As 8th row, change to Mercer-
Crochet.
12th row: As 5th row. (128 dc).
13th row: 1 dc into each dc, 1 ss into first dc.
14th row: 2 dc into same place as ss, * 1 dc
into each of next 15 dc, 2 dc into next dc;
repeat from * omitting 2 dc at end of last
repeat, 1 ss into first dc. (136 dc).
15th row: 1 dc into each dc, 1 ss into first dc.
16th row: As 15th row, change to health vest
cotton.
17th to 21st row: As 15th row.
22nd row: As 15th row, change to Mercer-
Crochet.
23rd row: Working into back loop only, 1 dc
into same place as ss, 1 dc into each of next
2 dc, * 2 dc into next dc, 1 dc into each of next
3 dc; repeat from * omitting 3 dc at end of last
repeat, 1 ss into first dc (170 dc).
24th to 26th row: As 15th row.
27th row: 1 dc into same place as ss, * 1 dc
into each of next 19 dc, (insert hook into next
dc and draw thread through) twice, thread
over and draw through all loops on hook – a
decrease made; repeat from * ending with 1 dc
into next dc, 1 ss into first dc. (162 dc).
28th and 29th rows: 1 dc into each st, 1 ss
into first st.
30th row: 1 dc into same place as ss, * 1 dc
into each of next 18 dc, a dec over next 2 dc;
repeat from * ending with 1 dc into next dc,
1 ss into first dc. (154 dc).
31st and 32nd rows: As 28th row.
33rd row: 1 dc into same place as ss, * 1 dc
into each of next 17 dc, a dec over next 2 dc;
repeat from * ending with 1 dc into next dc, 1
ss into first dc. (146 dc).
34th and 35th rows: As 28th row.
36th row: 1 dc into same place as ss, * 1 dc
into each of next 16 dc, a dec over next 2 dc;
repeat from * ending with 1 dc into next dc,

1 ss into first dc. (138 dc).
37th and 38th rows: As 28th row.
Fasten off.

Skip

1st row: Using health vest cotton and working over health vest cotton attach yarn to next dc, 1 dc into same place as join, 1 dc into each of next 55 dc, 1 ch, turn.
2nd row: Miss first dc, a dec over next 2 dc, 1 dc into each dc to within last 3 dc, a dec over next 2 dc, 1 ch, turn.
3rd row: Miss first st, a dec over next 2 dc, 1 dc into each dc to within last 3 sts, a dec over next 2 dc, 1 ch, turn.
Repeat 3rd row 4 times more.
8th row: Miss first st, (a dec over next 2 dc) twice, 1 dc into each dc to within last 5 dc, (a dec over next 2 dc) twice, turn.
9th row: 1 ss into each of first 2 sts, (a dec over next 2 dc) twice, 1 dc into each dc to within last 6 sts, (a dec over next 2 dc) twice, turn.
10th row: 1 ss into each of first 2 sts, a dec over next 2 dc, 1 dc into each dc to within last 4 sts, a dec over next 2 dc, 1 ch, turn.
11th row: Miss first st, a dec over next 2 dc, 1 dc into each dc to within last 3 sts, a dec over next 2 dc, 1 ss into next st. Fasten off.

Skip edging

With right side facing, using health vest cotton and working over health vest cotton, attach yarn to free dc before skip and work a row of dc neatly round skip ending with 1 ss into first free dc after skip. Fasten off.

Crown

Using Mercer-Crochet and working over elastic, attach thread to same place as last ss, 1 dc into each dc, ending with 1 ss into same place as join of skip edging. Fasten off.

Braid trimming

Using health vest cotton, commence with 2 ch, holding this between finger and thumb of left hand, work 1 dc into 2nd ch from hook, turn, inserting hook into back of loop, work 1 dc into foundation loop of 2nd ch made, * turn, insert hook into 2 loops at side, thread over and draw through 2 loops, thread over and draw through remaining 2 loops; repeat from * for 13½ ins or length required. Fasten off.
Damp and press.

To make up

½ in seam allowance has been given.
Cut two circles in lining and one in interlining 10 ins in diameter for top and two crosswise strips in lining and one in interlining 3½ × 30 ins for side band.
Place interlining to wrong side of one lining section of top and baste. Stitch short ends of crosscut lining and interlining strips. Place interlining to wrong side of one lining strip and baste (this forms side band). Baste side band to outer edge of top, if necessary stretching slightly, stitch in place. Dart lower edge to fit side band of cap. Stitch remaining lining sections in same manner. Place right sides of two completed sections together and stitch round outer edge, leaving an opening. Trim seams, turn to right side and slipstitch opening. Insert to wrong side of crochet and stitch in position, sew braid trimming as shown in illustration.

Beach bag

Materials: Coats 'Musica' health vest cotton 2 oz.
Ready-wound balls, 8 balls.
Milward disc (aluminium) crochet hook 4·00 (no. 8), or size to fit tension (gauge).
Piece of cardboard $6\frac{1}{2} \times 16$ ins.
$1\frac{1}{2}$ yds plastic lining 36 ins wide.
$1\frac{1}{2}$ yds bonded fibre interlining 32 ins wide.

Tension (gauge):
Size of motif – 3 ins square.
First 3 rows of main section – 1 in.

Measurement: Depth of bag – $15\frac{1}{2}$ ins approximately.

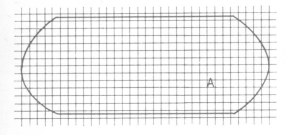

A – Base (cut 1 in cardboard).   1 sq = $\frac{1}{2}$ in

Motif band
First motif

Commence with 4 ch, join with a ss to form a ring.
1st row: 8 dc into ring. 1 ss into first dc.
2nd row: 5 ch, 1 hlf tr into same place as ss, 4 hlf tr into next dc, remove loop from hook, insert hook into first hlf tr of treble group and draw dropped loop through – a popcorn st made, * into next dc work 1 hlf tr 3 ch and 1 hlf tr, a popcorn st into next dc; repeat from * ending with 1 ss into 2nd of 5 ch.
3rd row: 1 dc into same place as ss, * 3 dc into next loop, 1 dc into next hlf tr, 1 dc into next popcorn st, 1 dc into next hlf tr; repeat from * omitting 1 dc at end of last repeat, 1 ss into first dc.
4th row: 2 ch, 1 hlf tr into next dc, * into next dc work 1 hlf tr 2 ch and 1 hlf tr, 1 hlf tr into each of next 5 dc; repeat from * omitting 2 hlf tr at end of last repeat, 1 ss into 2nd of 2 ch.
5th row: 1 dc into same place as ss, 1 dc into each of next 2 hlf tr, * 3 dc into next loop, 1 dc into each of next 7 hlf tr, repeat from * omitting 3 dc at end of last repeat, 1 ss into first dc. Fasten off.

Second motif

Work as first motif for 4 rows.
5th row: 1 dc into same place as ss, 1 dc into each of next 2 hlf tr, 1 dc into next loop, remove loop from hook, insert hook into centre dc of any corner on first motif and draw dropped loop through, 1 dc into same loop on second motif, remove loop from hook, insert hook into next dc on first motif and draw dropped loop through, 1 dc into same

loop on second motif, (remove loop from hook, insert hook into next dc on first motif and draw dropped loop through, 1 dc into next hlf tr on second motif) 7 times, remove loop from hook, insert hook into next dc on first motif and draw dropped loop through, 1 dc into next loop on second motif, join to next dc on first motif as before, 2 dc into same loop on second motif and complete as first motif.

Make 10 more motifs joining each as second motif was joined to first having 2 sides free on each side of joining and joining last motif to first motif.

Main section

1st row: With wrong side of motif band facing attach thread to join of any motifs, 1 dc into same place as join, * 1 dc into each of next 9 dc, 1 dc into next join of motifs; repeat from * omitting 1 dc at end of last repeat, 1 ss into first dc, turn.

2nd row: 1 ss into next dc, 2 ch, 3 hlf tr into same place as ss, remove loop from hook, insert hook into 2nd of 2 ch and draw dropped loop through (a starting popcorn st made), * 1 hlf tr into each of next 9 dc, a popcorn st into next dc; repeat from * omitting a popcorn st at end of last repeat, 1 ss into starting popcorn st, turn.

3rd row: 1 ss into next hlf tr, 1 dc into each st, 1 ss into first dc, turn.

4th row: 1 ss into next dc, 2 ch, 1 hlf tr into each of next 4 dc, * a popcorn st into next dc, 1 hlf tr into each of next 9 dc; repeat from * omitting 5 hlf tr at end of last repeat, 1 ss into 2nd of 2 ch, turn.

5th row: As 3rd row.

2nd to 5th row forms pattern.

Work in pattern until main section measures $12\frac{1}{2}$ ins approximately. Fasten off.

Base

Commence with 38 ch.

1st row: 1 tr into 4th ch from hook, 1 tr into each of next 33 ch, 7 tr into next ch, working along opposite side of foundation ch, 1 tr into each of next 34 ch, 6 tr into next ch, 1 ss into last foundation ch made.

2nd row: 3 ch, 1 tr into each of next 35 tr, 2 tr into each of next 5 tr, 1 tr into each of next 36 tr, 2 tr into each of next 5 tr, 1 ss into 3rd of 3 ch.

3rd row: 3 ch, 1 tr into each tr, 1 ss into 3rd of 3 ch.

4th row: 3 ch, 1 tr into each of next 35 tr, 2 tr into each of next 10 tr, 1 tr into each of next 36 tr, 2 tr into each of next 10 tr, 1 ss into 3rd of 3 ch.

5th row: As 3rd row.

6th row: 3 ch, 1 tr into each of next 35 tr, (2 tr into next tr, 1 tr into next tr) 10 times, 1 tr into each of next 36 tr, (2 tr into next tr, 1 tr into next tr) 10 times, 1 ss into 3rd of 3 ch.

7th row: As 3rd row. Fasten off.

Handle *make 2*

Commence with 6 ch, join with a ss to form a ring.

1st row: 1 dc into same place as ss, 1 dc into each ch.

Working in continuous rows, work 1 dc round stem of each dc until work measures 16 ins or length required. Fasten off.

To make up

$\frac{1}{2}$ in seam allowance has been given.

Cut two pieces of lining and one piece interlining 40×15 ins for side. Using cardboard for shape, cut two pieces of lining $7\frac{1}{2} \times 17\frac{1}{2}$ ins for base.

Place interlining to one piece of lining for side and baste in position. Having interlining to outside, place short ends together and machine stitch. Flatten seam and catch stitch seam allowance to interlining. Stitch one piece of lining for base in position. Turn to right side. Turn seam allowance at top to wrong side and catch stitch to interlining. Omitting interlining at catch stitching, complete another section in same manner. Insert, placing cardboard in position between two sections. Turn in top edge to wrong side and slipstitch.

Insert lining to crochet section and stitch in position round top edge. Place handles in position and sew securely.

Crochet for children

Child's pinafore dress

Materials: Of double knitting yarn,
7/8/9 (1 oz) balls in Main Shade and 1 (1 oz)
ball each in 2 contrast Shades.
No. 8 (4·00 mm) crochet hook, or size to fit
tension (gauge).

Measurements: To fit 22/24/26 ins chest;
length from top of shoulders, 16/18/20 ins.

Tension (gauge): 17 sts and 13 rows
measured over 4 ins of h tr, using no. 8 hook,
or size to fit tension (gauge).

Abbreviations: lp=loop; Decr 1=yarn
round hook, draw loop through each of next
2 sts, yrh, draw loop through all 4 loops on
hook.
D=Main Shade, M=1st Contrast, L=2nd
Contrast.

Front
* * with D, make 69/74/79 ch.
Foundation row: 1 hlf tr in 3rd ch from hook,
1 hlf tr in each ch to end, 68/73/78 sts.
Next row: 2 ch, miss 1st st, 1 hlf tr in each st
ending with 1 hlf tr in 2nd of 2 ch; the last row
forms pattern, rep it 4/5/6 times more.
Continue in hlf tr shaping skirt as follows:
Next row: 2 ch, 1 hlf tr in each of next 4/5/6
sts, Decr 1, 1 hlf tr in each of next 15/16/17 sts,
Decr 1, 1 hlf tr in each of next 20/21/22 sts,
Decr 1, 1 hlf tr in each of next 15/16/17 sts,
Decr 1, 1 hlf tr in each of last 4/5/6 sts, 1 hlf tr
in 2nd of 2 ch; 64/69/74 sts.
Work 3 rows straight.
Next row: 2 ch, 1 hlf tr in each of next 4/5/6
sts, Decr 1, 1 hlf tr in each of next 14/15/16 sts,
Decr 1, 1 hlf tr in each of next 18/19/20 sts,
Decr 1, 1 hlf tr in each of next 14/15/16 sts, Decr
1, 1 hlf tr in each of last 4/5/6 sts, 1 hlf tr in
2nd of 2 ch; 60/65/70 sts.

Work 3 rows straight.
Next row: 2 ch, 1 hlf tr in each of next 4/5/6
sts, Decr 1, 1 hlf tr in each of next 13/14/15 sts,
Decr 1, 1 hlf tr in each of next 16/17/18 sts,
Decr 1, 1 hlf tr in each of next 13/14/15 sts,
Decr 1, 1 hlf tr in each of last 4/5/6 sts, 1 hlf tr
in 2nd of 2 ch; 56/61/66 sts.
Work 3 rows straight.
Continue decreasing 4 sts thus on next and
following 4th row; 48/53/58 sts * *.
Work a few rows straight until front measures
7½/9/10½ ins at centre from start.
Divide for neck as follows:
Next row: 2 ch, 1 hlf tr in each of next
19/21/23 sts, turn and leave remaining sts
unworked.
1st row: Ss over 1 st, 2 ch, pattern to end.
2nd row: Pattern to turning ch, turn leaving
last st unworked.
3rd row: As 1st. Work 1 row straight. Rep last
2 rows twice more, then 1st row again;
14/16/18 sts.
Shape armhole as follows:
1st row: Ss over 3/4/5 sts, 2 ch, pattern to end.
2nd row: Pattern to turning ch, turn leaving
last st unworked.
3rd row: Ss over 1 st, 2 ch, pattern to end.
Rep last 2 rows once more, then 2nd row
again: 6/7/8 sts. Work straight until front
measures 15½/17½/19½ ins at centre from start,
ending at armhole edge.
Shape shoulder as follows:
Next row: Ss over 3/3/4 sts, 1 dc in each of
next 2/3/3 sts, 1 dc in 2nd of 2 ch. Fasten off.
With right side facing, leave centre 8/9/10 sts
unworked, rejoin yarn in next st and make 2
ch, pattern to end.
1st row: Pattern to turning ch, turn leaving
last st unworked.
2nd row: Ss over 1 st, 2 ch, pattern to end.

3rd row: As 1st. Work 1 row straight. Rep last 2 rows twice more, then 1st row again: 14/16/18 sts.

Shape armhole as follows:

1st row: Pattern to last 3/4/5 sts, turn leaving these sts unworked.

2nd row: Ss over 1st, 2 ch, pattern to end.

3rd row: Pattern to turning ch, turn leaving last st unworked. Rep 2nd and 3rd rows once more, then 2nd row again; 6/7/8 sts.

Work straight until front measures

$15\frac{1}{2}/17\frac{1}{2}/19\frac{1}{2}$ ins from start, ending at front edge.

Shape shoulder as follows:

Next row: 1 dc in each of first 3/4/4 sts. Fasten off.

Back

Work as for front from * * to * *. Work straight until back matches front at side edge. Shape armholes as follows:

Next row: SS over 3/4/5 sts, 2 ch, pattern to last 3/4/5 sts, turn leaving these sts unworked.

Next row: Ss over 1 st, 2 ch, pattern to turning ch, turn leaving last st unworked. Rep last row 4 times more; 32/35/38 sts.

Work straight until back matches front at armhole edge.

Shape shoulders as follows:

Next row: Ss over 3/3/4 sts, 1 dc in each of

next 3/4/4 sts, 1 hlf tr in each of next 20/21/22 sts, 1 dc in each of next 3/4/4 sts. Fasten off.

Pocket

With D, make 21 ch and work Foundation row as for front: 20 sts. Continue in hlf tr as for front and work a further 16 rows straight. Work border as follows:

1st row: * 4 ch, miss 3 sts, ss in next st; rep from * to end.

2nd row: * (1 dc, 1 hlf tr, 1 tr, 1 hlf tr, 1 dc) in ch sp, ss in same st as ss of previous row; rep from * to end. Fasten off.

Make another one the same.

Motif

With M, make 5 ch, join with ss to form a ring.

1st round: In M, 12 dc into ring. Join in L and join with ss in L in 1st dc.

2nd round: In L, * 5 ch, miss 1 st, ss in next st; rep from * ending with 2 ch, 1 tr in base of 5 ch.

3rd round: In L, * 5 ch, ss in 3rd of 5 ch of previous round; rep from * all round. Join with ss in M in 1st of 5 ch.

4th round: In M, * (1 dc, 1 hlf tr, 1 tr, 2 ch, 1 tr, 1 hlf tr, 1 dc) in 5 ch sp, ss in ss of previous round, 9 ch, ss in same st; rep from * all round, ending with (3 ch, 1 dbl tr) in last ss.

5th round: In L, * 4 ch, 1 dc in 2 ch sp, 4 ch, 1 dc in 9 ch lp; rep from * ending with 1 dc in lp.

6th round: In L, * (1 dc, 1 hlf tr, 2 tr, 1 hlf tr, 1 dc) in 4 ch sp; rep from * all round. Join with ss in 1st dc. Fasten off. Make another one the same.

To make up

Using a warm iron and damp cloth, press parts lightly on wrong side. Join right shoulder seam.

Neck border

With right side facing and D, work 1 row dc all round neck, then work 1st and 2nd rows of border as for pocket. Fasten off.

Join right shoulder seam, then work round armholes as for neck border. Join side seams, then with wrong side facing, work 1st row of border all round lower edge, turn and work 2nd row. Fasten off.

Sew motif in centre of each pocket. Pin pockets on front of dress, $1/1\frac{1}{2}/2$ ins in from side seams, and immediately above border sew in position. Press all seams and borders lightly.

Pyjama case

for colour illustration, see page 77

A – *Front (cut 1)*
B – *Ear (cut 4 from fabric and 2 from inter-*
lining)
C – *Back (cut 2)*

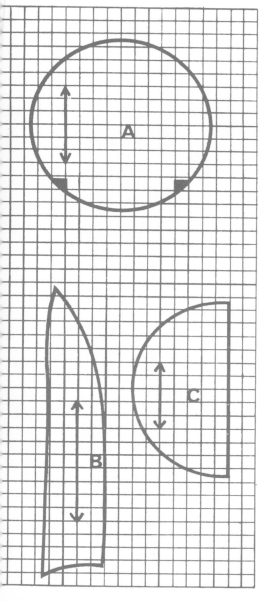

Materials: Coats Mercer-Crochet no. 20
(20 grms).
1 ball.
This model is worked in shade 510 (Cobalt
Blue), but any other shade of Mercer-Crochet
may be used.
Milward steel crochet hook no. 3 (1·25 mm), or
size to fit tension (gauge).
$\frac{5}{8}$ yd fabric 36 ins wide.
Piece of interlining for ears.
10 ins. 'Lightning' Gold Pack (nylon) zip.
A cushion pad (optional).

Tension (gauge): Size of motif=$1\frac{1}{8}$ ins
square.

Measurements: Finished size of case=12 ins
diameter.

Motif *make 3*
Commence with 5 ch.
1st row: Leaving the last loop of each on
hook work 2 dbl tr into 5th ch from hook,
thread over and draw through all loops on
hook (a 2 dbl tr cluster made), (5 ch, a 3 dbl tr
cluster into same place as last cluster) 3 times,
5 ch, 1 ss into first cluster.
2nd row: 8 ch, 1 tr into same place as ss, (4 ch,
into next cluster work 1 tr 5 ch and 1 tr) 3
times, 4 ch, 1 ss into 3rd of 8 ch.
3rd row: 1 ss into next loop, 3 ch, into same
loop work 3 tr 1 dbl tr 3 ch 1 dbl tr and 4 tr,
(into next 4 ch loop work 2 dc 2 ch and 2 dc,
into next 5 ch loop work 4 tr 1 dbl tr 3 ch 1 dbl
tr and 4 tr) 3 times, into next 4 ch loop work 2
dc 2 ch and 2 dc, 1 ss into 3rd of 3 ch. Fasten
off.

Motif strip *make 2*
First motif
Work motif as before.

Second motif

Work as first motif for 2 rows.

3rd row: 1 ss into next loop, 3 ch, into same
loop work 3 tr 1 dbl tr and 1 ch, 1 dc into any
3 ch loop on first motif, 1 ch, into same loop on
second motif work 1 dbl tr and 4 tr and complete as first motif.

Make 5 more motifs joining each as second
motif was joined to first, leaving 1 point free
on each side between joinings.

Trimming for ear *make 2*

Commence with 5 ch.

1st row: * 1 tr into 5th ch from hook, 5 ch;
repeat from * for 31 ins or length required,
ending with 1 tr into 5th ch from hook, 1 ch.

2nd row: 2 dc over last tr worked, * 2 ch, 2
dc over next tr, repeat from * ending with 1 ss
into first ch worked. Fasten off.

Eyebrow *make 2*

Work as trimming for ear for 5 ins.

Mouth

Work as trimming for ear for 6 ins.

To make up

⅝ in seam allowance has been given on all
pieces.

Stitch zip in position to straight edges of back
sections.

Place ear sections right sides together and
interlining to one side. Stitch leaving short
ends open. Turn to right side.

Stitch ears in position to front *(see illustration)*.

Stitch front to back, right sides together. Turn
to right side.

Place motifs and trimming on front to form
features and sew in position. Sew on length of
trimming to edge of each ear. Sew one strip of
motifs centrally to right side of each ear.

Baby's shawl

Materials: 24 (25 grms) balls 3-ply yarn. No. 9 (3·50 mm) crochet hook, or size to fit tension (gauge).

Measurement: 52 ins square.

Tension (gauge): Each motif measures 7¼ ins square.

Abbreviations: Cl=cluster worked as follows: Yarn round hook, (insert hook in sp and draw a loop through, yarn round hook) 4 times, draw loop through all 9 loops on hook, draw loop through last loop.

Motif

Make 5 ch. Join with ss to form a ring.
1st round: 2 ch, 11 tr into ring. Join with ss in 2nd of 2 ch.
2nd round: 4 ch, 1 tr in same st, * 1 tr in next st, 1 ch, 1 tr in next st, (1 tr, 2 ch, 1 tr) in next st; rep from * twice, 1 tr in next st, 1 ch, 1 tr in last st. Join with ss in 2nd of 4 ch.
3rd round: (Ss, 4 ch, 3 tr) in 1st ch sp, * 1 ch, Cl in next ch sp, 1 ch, (3 tr, 2 ch, 3 tr) in next ch sp; rep from * twice, 1 ch, Cl in last ch sp, 1 ch, 2 tr in 1st ch sp, join with ss in 2nd of 4 ch.
4th round: (Ss, 4 ch, 3 tr) in 1st ch sp, * (1 ch, Cl in next ch sp) twice, 1 ch, (3 tr, 2 ch, 3 tr) in next ch sp; rep from * twice, (1 ch, Cl in next ch sp) twice, 1 ch, 2 tr in 1st ch sp. Join with ss in 2nd of 4 ch.
5th round: (Ss, 4 ch, 3 tr) in 1st ch sp, * (1 ch, Cl in next ch sp) 3 times, 1 ch, (3 tr, 2 ch, 3 tr) in next ch sp; rep from * twice, (1 ch, Cl in next ch sp) 3 times, 1 ch, 2 tr in 1st ch sp; join with ss in 2nd of 4 ch.
6th round: (Ss, 4 ch, 3 tr) in 1st ch sp, * (1 ch, Cl in next ch sp) 4 times, 1 ch, (3 tr, 2 ch, 3 tr) in next ch sp; rep from * twice, (1 ch, Cl in next ch sp) 4 times, 1 ch, 2 tr in 1st ch sp. Join with ss in 2nd of 4 ch.
7th round: (Ss, 4 ch, 3 tr) in 1st ch sp, * (1 ch, Cl in next ch sp) 5 times, 1 ch, (3 tr, 2 ch, 3 tr) in next ch sp; rep from * twice, (1 ch, Cl in next ch sp) 5 times, 1 ch, 2 tr in 1st ch sp. Join with ss in 2nd of 2 ch.
8th round: (Ss, 4 ch, 3 tr) in 1st ch sp, * (1 ch, Cl in next ch sp) 6 times, 1 ch, (3 tr, 2 ch, 3 tr) in next ch sp; rep from * twice, (1 ch, Cl in next ch sp) 6 times, 1 ch, 2 tr in 1st ch sp. Join with ss in 2nd of 4 ch.
9th round: (Ss, 4 ch, 3 tr) in 1st ch sp, * (1 ch, Cl in next ch sp) 7 times, 1 ch, (3 tr, 2 ch, 3 tr) in next ch sp; rep from * twice, (1 ch, Cl in next ch sp) 7 times, 1 ch, 2 tr in 1st ch sp. Join with ss in 2nd of 4 ch.
10th round: (Ss, 4 ch, 3 tr) in 1st ch sp, * (1 ch, Cl in next ch sp) 8 times, 1 ch, (3 tr, 2 ch, 3 tr) in next ch sp; rep from * twice, (1 ch, Cl in next ch sp) 8 times, 1 ch, 2 tr in 1st ch sp. Join with ss in 2nd of 4 ch.
11th round: (Ss, 4 ch, 3 tr) in 1st ch sp, * (1 ch, Cl in next ch sp) 9 times, 1 ch, (3 tr, 2 ch, 3 tr) in next ch sp; rep from * twice, (1 ch, Cl in next ch sp) 9 times, 1 ch, 2 tr in 1st ch sp. Join with ss in 2nd of 4 ch. Fasten off.
Make another 48 squares the same.
Make a strip 7 motifs long, joining motifs together as follows: Place 2 motifs right sides together, and with wrong side facing rejoin yarn in corner sp, then work across the 2 motifs in dc, working 1 dc in each tr, 1 dc in each ch sp, and 1 dc in top of each Cl.

Make a further 6 strips thus, then join the long strips together in the same way.

Border

With right side facing, rejoin yarn in corner sp and make 4 ch, 3 tr in same sp, * (3 tr, 2 ch, 1 dc in 2nd ch from hook, 3 tr) in top of next Cl, miss next Cl; rep from * 4 times more, then work same shell in join of squares; rep from * all round working a shell in each corner sp and ending with 2 tr in 1st corner sp. Join with ss in 2nd of 4 ch. Fasten off.

To make up

Using a warm iron and damp cloth, block and press work lightly on wrong side. Darn in short ends of yarn.

Gifts to make

Cushion

for colour illustration, see page 81

Materials: Of double knitting yarn, 2 (1 oz) balls each in Purple and in Olive Green and 6 (1 oz) balls each in Turquoise and in Slate Blue.
No. 8 crochet hook (4.00 mm) or size to fit tension (gauge). 18 ins zip.

Measurements: Cushion measures 21 ins in diameter.

Abbreviations: Decr 1=(yarn round hook, draw loop through next st, yrh, draw loop through 2 loops) twice, yarn round hook, draw loop through all 3 loops on hook.
P=Purple. T=Turquoise. G=Olive Green. B=Slate Blue.

With P, make 4 ch, join with ss to form a ring.
1st round: 2 ch, 11 tr into ring, 12 sts, join with ss in 2nd of 2 ch.
2nd round: 2 ch, * 2 tr in next st, rep from * ending with 1 tr in base of 2 ch, 24 sts, join with ss.
3rd round: 2 ch, * 2 tr in next st, 1 tr in next st, rep from * ending with 2 tr in last st, 36 sts, join with ss.
4th round: 2 ch, * 2 tr in next st, 1 tr in each of next 2 sts, rep from * ending with 1 tr in last st, 48 sts, join with ss.
5th round: 2 ch, * 2 tr in next st, 1 tr in each of next 3 sts, rep from * ending with 1 tr in each of last 2 sts, 60 sts, join with ss.
6th round: 2 ch, * 2 tr in next st, 1 tr in each of next 4 sts, rep from * ending with 1 tr in each of last 3 sts, 72 sts, join with ss.
7th round: 2 ch, * 2 tr in next st, 1 tr in each of next 5 sts, rep from * ending with 1 tr in each of last 4 sts, 84 sts, join with ss.
8th round: 2 ch, * 2 tr in next st, 1 tr in each of next 6 sts, rep from * ending with 1 tr in each of last 5 sts, 96 sts, join with ss.

9th round: 2 ch, * 2 tr in next st, 1 tr in each of next 7 sts, rep from * ending with 1 tr in each of last 6 sts, 108 sts, join with ss.
10th round: 2 ch, * 2 tr in next st, 1 tr in each of next 8 sts, rep from * ending with 1 tr in each of last 7 sts, 120 sts, join with ss.
Join in T and make 2 ch, 1 tr in same st, 1 tr in each of next 17 sts, 2 tr in next st, turn; continue on these 21 sts for petal as follows:
Next row: 2 ch, 1 tr in 1st st, 1 tr in each st to turning ch, 2 tr in 2nd of 2 ch, turn, rep last row twice more, 27 sts.
Next row: 2 ch, miss 1st st, 1 tr in each st ending with 1 tr in 2nd of 2 ch, rep last row 3 times more.
Next row: 2 ch, decr 1, 1 tr in each st to last 3 sts, decr 1, 1 tr in 2nd of 2 ch, rep last row 3 times more, 19 sts.
Next row: 3 ch, (Decr 1) twice, 1 tr in each st to last 5 sts, (Decr 1) twice, 1 dbl tr in top of turning ch, rep. last row twice more, 7 sts.
Next row: 2 ch, Decr 1, 1 tr in next st, Decr 1, 1 tr in 3rd of 3 ch, 5 sts.
Next row: 2 ch, (yrh, draw loop through next st, yrh, draw through 2 loops) 3 times, yrh, draw loop through 2nd of 2 ch, yrh, draw through 2 loops, yrh, draw loop through all 5 loops on hook. Fasten off.
With right side facing, leave next st unworked, rejoin T in next st and work remaining 5 petals to correspond.

Infill panel
Join in G in unworked st between petals and make 2 ch, ss in tr of adjacent row of petal, then work 1 tr in same st, 2 sts, join with ss in 2nd of 2 ch of adjacent row of petal, turn.
Next row: 2 ch, ss in tr of adjacent row of petal, 1 tr in 2nd of 2 ch, ss in 2nd of 2 ch of adjacent row of petal, turn, rep last row twice more.

Joining beg and end of row to petals thus, continue as follows: Next row: 2 ch, ss in tr of petal, 1 tr in base of 2 ch, 2 tr in 2nd of 2 ch, join with ss in 2 ch of petal, 4 sts.

Next row: 2 ch, ss in tr of petal, 1 tr in base of these 2 ch, 1 tr in each st ending with 2 tr in 2nd of 2 ch, join with ss in 2 ch of petal, rep last row twice more, 10 sts.

Next row: 2 ch, ss in tr of petal, 1 tr in base of these 2 ch, 2 tr in next st, 1 tr in each st to last 2 sts, 2 tr in next st, 2 tr in 2nd of 2 ch, join with ss in 2 ch of petal, 14 sts, rep last row 3 times more, 26 sts. Break G. Join in B.

Next row: in B, 2 ch, ss in tr of petal, 1 tr in base of these 2 ch, (2 tr in next st) twice, 1 tr in each st to last 3 sts, (2 tr in next st) twice, 2 tr in 2nd of 2 ch, 32 sts, join with ss in 2 ch of petal, rep last row twice more, 44 sts.

Next row: 2 ch, ss in tr of petal, 1 tr in base of these 2 ch, 2 tr in next tr, 1 tr in each st to last 2 sts, 2 tr in next st, 2 tr in 2nd of 2 ch, 48 sts, join with ss in 2 ch of petal. Break B.

Work remaining 5 infill panels between petals to correspond, but leave yarn unbroken on last panel, turn.

Next round: right side facing, 3 ch, 1 tr in next tr, * 1 tr in each of next 10 tr, 2 tr in next tr, 1 tr in each of next 23 tr, 2 tr in next tr, 1 tr in each of last 11 tr, 1 dbl tr in 2nd of 2 ch, 1 dbl tr in 1st st of next panel, rep from * all round, ending with 1 dbl tr in 2nd of 2 ch of last panel, join with ss in 3rd of 3 ch. Make another circle the same.

Gusset
With B, make 301 ch.

Foundation row: 1 tr in 3rd ch from hook, 1 tr in each ch to end, 300 sts.

Next row: 2 ch, miss 1st st, 1 tr in each st ending with 1 tr in 2nd of 2 ch. Rep this row 4 times more. Fasten off.

To make up
Using a warm iron and damp cloth, press parts lightly on wrong side. Darn in short ends of yarn neatly.

Join short ends of gusset together, then with wrong side of cushion facing, place gusset on top of work and crochet gusset and circle together in dc. Fasten off.

Pin zip between gusset and 2nd circle; sew in position, then with wrong side of cushion facing, join remainder of cushion together in the same way.

80

Spectacle case

for colour illustration, see frontispiece

Materials: Coats Mercer-Crochet no. 20 (20 grms). 1 ball.
This model is worked in 612 (Lt Amethyst), but any other shade of Mercer-Crochet may be used.
Milward steel crochet hook 1·25 (no. 3), or size to fit tension (gauge).
⅛ yd fabric 36 ins wide in contrasting colour.
⅛ yd bonded fibre interlining.
Spectacle case frame.

Tension (gauge):
8 rows = 1½ ins approximately.
1 pattern = 1¼ ins.

Measurements: 6½ × 3¾ ins

Side section, *make 2*
Commence with 35 ch.
1st row: 1 dc into 2nd ch from hook, * 6 ch, miss 5 ch, 1 dc into next ch, 3 ch, miss 2 ch, 1 dc into next ch; repeat from * ending with 6 ch, miss 5 ch, 1 dc into next ch, 3 ch, turn.
2nd row: 1 tr into next loop, 3 ch, 1 dc into last tr – a picot made – into same loop work (2 tr, a picot) 3 times and 1 tr, * 1 dc into next loop, into next loop work (2 tr, a picot) 5 times and 1 tr; repeat from * to within last loop, into next loop work (2 tr, a picot) 4 times, 1 tr into next dc, 1 ch, turn.
3rd row: 1 dc into next picot, * 6 ch, miss 1 picot, 1 dc into next picot, 6 ch, miss 2 picots, 1 dc into next picot; repeat from * ending with 6 ch, miss 1 picot, 1 dc into next picot, 1 ch, turn.
4th row: 1 dc into first dc, * into next loop work (2 dc, a picot) twice and 2 dc, into next loop work (2 tr, a picot) 5 times and 1 tr; repeat from * ending with, into next loop work (2 dc, a picot) twice and 2 dc, 1 dc into next dc, turn.
5th row: 1 ss into each of first 3 dc, 1 dc into next picot, 6 ch, miss 2 picots, 1 dc into next picot, * 6 ch, miss 1 picot, 1 dc into next picot.

6 ch, miss 4 picots, 1 dc into next picot, repeat from * ending with 6 ch, miss 2 picots, 1 dc into next picot, 3 ch, turn.
6th row: 1 tr into first loop, a picot, into same loop work (2 tr, a picot) 3 times and 1 tr, * into next loop work (2 dc, a picot) twice and 2 dc, into next loop work (2 tr, a picot) 5 times and 1 tr; repeat from * to within last loop, into next loop work (2 tr, a picot) 4 times, 1 tr into next dc, 1 ch, turn.
7th row: 1 dc into next picot, * 6 ch, miss 1 picot, 1 dc into next picot, 6 ch, miss 4 picots, 1 dc into next picot; repeat from * ending with 6 ch, miss 1 picot, 1 dc into next picot, 1 ch, turn.
4th to 7th row forms pattern. Continue in pattern until work measures 6 ins or length required ending with a 5th pattern row and turning with 1 ch.
Next row: 1 dc into first dc, * 6 dc into next loop, 1 dc into next dc; repeat from * to end. Fasten off.

Joining
Place wrong sides together and working through both sections, attach thread to row end 1¼ ins from top edge, 1 dc into same place as join, work a row of dc evenly all round working 3 dc into each corner and ending at corresponding row end on second side.
Fasten off.
Damp and pin out to measurements.

To make up
Cut 4 pieces of fabric and 2 pieces of interlining 7¼ × 4½ ins, ½ in seam allowance has been given on all pieces.
(Lining should be machine stitched ⅝ in from the edge.)
Baste 2 pieces of fabric right sides together and machine stitch leaving 1 short side open and 1¼ ins free on each long side for top opening. Trim seams and press. This forms the lining.
Baste 1 piece of interlining to wrong side of one remaining fabric section. Baste another piece in same manner. With right sides of fabric together, machine stitch as lining. Trim seams, press and turn to right side.
Insert lining.
Slip crochet over fabric and secure.
Place frame to outside edge of opening, making 2 small pleats across top if required, and sew neatly to frame.

Luncheon mat and napkin

for colour illustration, see page 85

Materials: Coats Mercer-Crochet no. 10 (20 grms).

3 balls.

This model was worked in 524 (Dk Jade) any desired colour may be used.

No. 10 is available in White; 402 (Lt Rose Pink); 403 (Rose Pink); 439 (Rose Madder); 442 (Mid Buttercup); 463 (Parrot Green); 469 (Geranium); 503 (Coral Pink); 508 (Lt Marine Blue); 513 (Orange); 521 (Jade); 524 (Dk Jade); 538 (Marigold); 575 (Mid Laurel Green); 582 (Straw Yellow); 608 (Tussah); 609 (Ecru); 610 (Dk Ecru); 612 (Lt Amethyst); 621 (Lt French Blue); 623 (Spring Green); 625 (Lt Beige); 693 (Carnation Pink); 700 (Turkey Red); 761 (Lt Forget-me-not); 776 (Emerald Green); 795 (Amber Gold); 962 (Dk Buttercup); Spec 8918 (Lt Coral Pink).

Piece of linen 12½ ins square to match.

Milward steel crochet hook 1·50 (no. 2½), or size to fit tension (gauge).

Tension (gauge): First 3 rows = 2 ins diameter.

Measurements: Mat = 14 ins diameter. Napkin = 12 ins square.

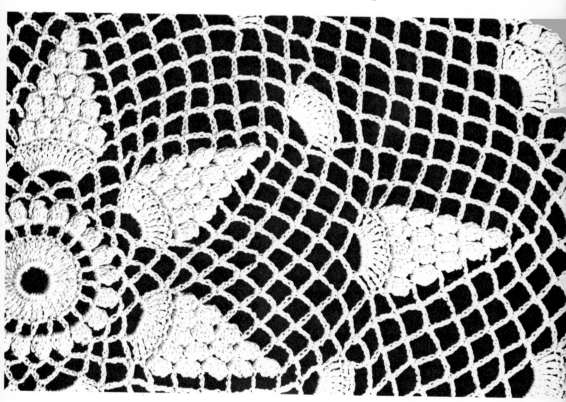

Luncheon mat

Commence with 12 ch, join with 1 ss to form a ring.

1st row: 4 ch, 41 dbl tr into ring, join with 1 ss into 4th of 4 ch.

2nd row: 5 ch, * miss 1 dbl tr, 1 tr into next dbl tr, 2 ch; repeat from * join with 1 ss into 3rd of 5 ch. (21 sps).

3rd row: 1 ss into first sp, 3 ch, 4 tr into same sp, drop loop from hook, insert hook into top of 3 ch, draw dropped loop through (popcorn st made), * 5 ch, 5 tr into next sp, drop loop from hook, insert hook into first tr, draw dropped loop through (another popcorn st made); repeat from * ending with 2 ch, 1 tr into top of first popcorn st.

4th row: * 6 ch, 1 dc into next loop; repeat from * ending with 3 ch, 1 tr into tr of previous row.

5th row: * 7 ch, 1 dc into next loop; repeat from * all round, ending with 3 ch, 1 dbl tr into tr of previous row.

6th row: * 7 ch, 1 dc into next loop, 11 dbl tr into next loop, 1 dc into next loop; repeat from * omitting 1 dc at end of last repeat, 1 ss into dbl tr of previous row.

7th row: 1 ss into centre of next loop, 1 dc into same loop, * 7 ch, 1 dc into next dbl tr, (2 ch, miss 1 dbl tr, 1 dc into next dbl tr) 5 times, 7 ch, 1 dc into next loop; repeat from * ending last repeat with 3 ch, 1 dbl tr into first dc.

8th row: 7 ch, 1 dc into next loop, * 7 ch, (1 popcorn st into next 2 ch loop, 2 ch) 4 times, 1 popcorn st into next 2 ch loop, (7 ch, 1 dc into next loop) twice; repeat from * omitting (7 ch and 1 dc) twice at end of last repeat, 3 ch, 1 dbl tr into dbl tr of previous row.

9th to 12th row: As 8th row, having 1 popcorn st less on each pineapple and 1 loop more between pineapples on each row. (1 popcorn st and 7 loops on 12th row).

13th to 15th row: * 7 ch, 1 dc into next loop; repeat from * ending with 3 ch, 1 dbl tr into dbl tr of previous row.

16th row: * 11 dbl tr into next loop, 1 dc into next loop, (7 ch, 1 dc into next loop) 5 times; repeat from * ending last repeat with 3 ch, 1 dbl tr into dbl tr of previous row.

17th row: * 7 ch, (1 dc into next dbl tr, 2 ch, miss next dbl tr) 5 times, 1 dc into next dbl tr, (7 ch, 1 dc into next loop) twice, 11 dbl tr into next loop, 1 dc into next loop, 7 ch, 1 dc into next loop; repeat from * ending last repeat with 3 ch, 1 dbl tr into dbl tr of previous row.

18th row: 7 ch, 1 dc into next loop, * (7 ch, miss 2 loops, 1 dc into next loop) twice, 7 ch, 1 dc into next loop, 7 ch, 1 dc into next dbl tr, (2 ch, miss 1 dbl tr, 1 dc into next dbl tr) 5 times, (7 ch, 1 dc into next loop) twice; repeat from * omitting (7 ch and 1 dc) twice at end of last repeat, 3 ch, 1 dbl tr into dbl tr of previous row.

19th row: (7 ch, 1 dc into next loop) 5 times, * 7 ch, (popcorn st into next loop, 2 ch) 4 times, popcorn st into next loop, (7 ch, 1 dc into next loop) 6 times; repeat from * omitting (7 ch and 1 dc) 6 times at end of last repeat, 3 ch, 1 dbl tr into dbl tr of previous row.

20th to 23rd row: As 19th row, having 1 popcorn st less on each pineapple and 1 loop more between pineapples on each row. (1 popcorn st and 11 loops on 23rd row).

24th to 26th row: * 7 ch, 1 dc into next loop; repeat from * ending with 3 ch, 1 dbl tr into dbl tr of previous row.

27th row: As 26th row increasing 3 loops evenly all round – increase work 1 dc 7 ch and 1 dc into same loop, join as before (80 loops).

28th row: * 11 dbl tr into next loop, 1 dc into next loop, (7 ch, 1 dc into next loop) twice; repeat from * omitting 7 ch and 1 dc at end of last repeat, 3 ch, 1 dbl tr into dbl tr of previous row.

29th row: * 3 ch, (1 dc into next dbl tr, 2 ch, miss next dbl tr) 5 times, 1 dc into next dbl tr, 3 ch, 1 dc into next loop, 7 ch, 1 dc into next loop; repeat from * omitting 1 dc at end of last repeat, 1 ss into dbl tr of previous row.

30th row: Ss into next loop, 1 dc into same loop, * (2 ch, popcorn st into next loop) 5 times, 2 ch, 1 dc into next loop, into next loop work (2 dc, 2 ch) 3 times and 2 dc, 1 dc into next loop; repeat from * omitting 1 dc at end of last repeat, 1 ss into first dc. Fasten off.

Napkin

Make a narrow hem to right side all round linen. Attach thread to any corner, 2 dc into same place, 3 ch, 1 dc into 3rd ch from hook (picot made), 2 dc into same place as last 2 dc, dc closely all round, working 8 dc to 1 in and making a picot after every 4th dc and working other corners in same manner, join with 1 ss into first dc. Fasten off.

Tissue, cotton wool & roller holder

for colour illustration, see page 89

Materials: Coats Mercer-Crochet no. 20 (20 grms).
2 balls for tissue holder.
2 balls for cotton wool holder.
3 balls for roller holder.
These models are worked in shade 621 (Lt French Blue), but any other shade of Mercer-Crochet may be used.
Milward steel crochet hook 1·25 (no. 3), or size to fit tension (gauge).
¾ yd fabric 36 ins wide in contrasting colour.
A cylindrical container 5½ × 4⅜ ins.

Tension:
Size of flower motif = 1 in approximately diameter.
First 2 rows of dbl tr = 1⅛ ins diameter.
5 rows of tr = 1 in.

Measurements:
Tissue holder = 10 × 4¾ × 2¾ ins.
Cotton wool holder
  Base = 4⅜ ins diameter.
  Side = 5½ ins
Roller holder
  Base = 6½ ins diameter.
  Side = 9¼ ins

Tissue holder

Side

Flower motifs
First motif
Commence with 8 ch, join with a ss to form a ring.
1st row: 20 dc into ring, 1 ss into first dc.
2nd row: 1 dc into same place as ss, (4 ch, miss 4 dc, 1 dc into next dc) 3 times, 4 ch, miss 4 dc, 1 ss into first dc.
3rd row: Into each loop work 1 dc 1 hlf tr 3 tr

1 hlf tr and 1 dc, 1 ss into first dc. (4 petals made.)
4th row: (5 ch, inserting hook from behind, work 1 dc into next dc on 2nd row) 3 times, 5 ch.
5th row: Into each loop work 1 dc 1 hlf tr 1 tr 3 dbl tr 1 tr 1 hlf tr and 1 dc, 1 ss into first dc. Fasten off.
Second motif
Work as first motif for 4 rows.
5th row: Into first loop work 1 dc 1 hlf tr 1 tr and 1 dbl tr, 1 ss into centre st of any petal on first motif, into same loop on second motif work 2 dbl tr 1 tr 1 hlf tr and 1 dc and complete as first motif.
Make 24 more motifs joining each as second motif was joined to first leaving 1 petal free between joinings and joining last motif to first motif to correspond.

Edging
1st row: With right side facing, attach thread to centre dbl tr of free petal on any motif, 1 dc into same place as join, * 6 ch, miss 6 sts, leaving the last loop of each on hook work 1 trip tr into next tr and 1 trip tr into corresponding tr on next petal, thread over and draw through all loops on hook (a joint trip tr made), 6 ch, 1 dc into centre dbl tr on next petal; repeat from * omitting 1 dc at end of last repeat, 1 ss into first dc.
2nd row: 1 ss into next ch, 4 ch, * (miss 1 ch, 1 tr into next ch, 1 ch) twice, miss 1 ch, 1 tr into next joint trip tr, (1 ch, miss 1 ch, 1 tr into next ch) 3 times, 1 ch, miss next dc, 1 tr into next ch, 1 ch; repeat from * omitting 1 tr and 1 ch at end of last repeat, 1 ss into 3rd of 4 ch.
3rd row: 4 ch, * 1 tr into next tr, 1 ch; repeat from * ending with 1 ss into 3rd of 4 ch.
Repeat 3rd row 3 times more.
7th row: 1 dc into same place as ss, * 1 dc into

next sp, 1 dc into next tr; repeat from * ending with 1 dc into next sp, 1 ss into first dc.

8th row: 1 dc into each dc, 1 ss into first dc. Fasten off.

Attach thread to opposite side of motifs and work as first side for 4 rows.

5th and 6th rows: As 7th and 8th rows of first side.

Top

Flower motifs

Make 8 motifs joining to form a strip.

Ninth motif

Work as second motif leaving 2 petals free at outside edge of previous motif.

Make 1 more motif joining as second motif was joined to first.

Make 1 more motif joining as 9th motif.

Make 6 more motifs joining as second motif was joined to first.

Make 1 more motif leaving 2 petals free at outside edge of previous motif and joining to first motif to correspond.

Heading

1st row: With right side facing, attach thread to centre dbl tr of free petal on any short side. 1 dc into same place as join, * * 6 ch, miss 6 sts, leaving the last loop of each on hook work 1 trip tr into next tr (1 dbl tr into corresponding tr on next petal) twice and 1 trip tr into corresponding tr on next petal, thread over and draw through all loops on hook (a joint st made at corner), * 6 ch, 1 dc into centre dbl tr of next petal, 6 ch, miss 6 sts, a joint trip tr over next 2 tr; repeat from * 4 times more, 6 ch, 1 dc into centre dbl tr of next petal, 6 ch, miss 6 sts, a joint st over next 4 tr, 6 ch, 1 dc into centre dbl tr of next petal; repeat from * * omitting 1 dc at end of repeat, 1 ss into first dc.

2nd row: 4 ch, * * miss 1 ch, 1 tr into next ch, 1 ch, miss 1 ch, 1 tr into next ch, miss 5 sts, 1 tr into next ch, 1 ch, miss 1 ch, 1 tr into next ch, 1 ch, miss 1 ch, 1 tr into next dc, * (1 ch, miss 1 ch, 1 tr into next ch) 3 times, 1 ch, miss 1 st, (1 tr into next ch, 1 ch, miss 1 ch) 3 times, 1 tr into next dc; repeat from * 4 times more, (1 ch, miss 1 ch, 1 tr into next ch) twice, miss 5 sts, 1 tr into next ch, 1 ch, miss 1 ch, 1 tr into next ch, 1 ch, miss 1 ch, 1 tr into next dc, 1 ch; repeat from * * omitting 1 tr and 1 ch at end of repeat, 1 ss into 3rd of 4 ch.

3rd row: 1 dc into same place as ss, * (1 dc

into next sp, 1 dc into next tr) twice, (1 dc into next tr, 1 dc into next sp) 39 times, 1 dc into each of next 2 tr, (1 dc into next sp, 1 dc into next tr) twice; repeat from * omitting 1 dc at end of repeat, 1 ss into first dc. Fasten off.

Edging

1st row: With right side facing, attach thread to centre dbl tr of free petal on any short side, 1 dc into same place as join, * 6 ch, miss 6 sts, a joint trip tr over next 2 tr, 6 ch, 1 dc into centre dbl tr of next petal, 6 ch, miss 1 st, a joint trip tr over next 2 tr, 6 ch, miss 1 st, 1 dc into next dbl tr, (6 ch, miss 6 sts a joint trip tr over next 2 tr, 6 ch, 1 dc into centre dbl tr of next petal) 7 times, 6 ch, miss 1 st, a joint trip tr over next 2 tr, 6 ch, miss 1 st, 1 dc into next dbl tr, 6 ch, miss 6 sts, a joint trip tr over next 2 tr, 6 ch, 1 dc into centre dbl tr of next petal; repeat from * omitting 1 dc at end of repeat, 1 ss into first dc.

2nd row: 1 ss into next ch, 4 ch, * (miss 1 ch, 1 tr into next ch, 1 ch) twice, miss 1 ch, 1 tr into next joint trip tr, (1 ch, miss 1 ch, 1 tr into next ch) 3 times, 1 ch, miss 1 dc, (1 tr into next ch, 1 ch, miss 1 ch) 3 times, into next joint trip tr work (1 tr, 1 ch) twice and 1 tr (a corner made), * * (1 ch, miss 1 ch, 1 tr into next ch) 3 times, 1 ch, miss 1 dc, (1 tr into next ch, 1 ch, miss 1 ch) 3 times, 1 tr into next joint trip tr; repeat from * * 7 times more, 1 ch, into same joint trip tr work 1 tr 1 ch and 1 tr (another corner made), (1 ch, miss 1 ch, 1 tr into next ch) 3 times, 1 ch, miss 1 dc, (1 tr into next ch, 1 ch, miss 1 ch) 3 times, 1 tr into next joint trip tr, (1 ch, miss 1 ch, 1 tr into next ch) 3 times, 1 ch, miss 1 dc, 1 tr into next ch; repeat from * omitting 1 tr at end of repeat, 1 ss into 3rd of 4 ch.

3rd to 5th row: 4 ch, * 1 tr into next tr, 1 ch; repeat from * working (1 tr, 1 ch) twice and 1 tr into centre tr at each corner, ending with 1 ss into 3rd of 4 ch.

6th row: As 7th row of edging for side.

7th row: As 8th row of edging for side decreasing 2 sts evenly spaced on each side – to decrease, (insert hook into next dc and draw thread through) twice, thread over and draw through all loops on hook.

Joining

Place wrong side of edging for side (2nd side) to wrong side of edging for top and working through last row of each piece, 1 dc into each st, 1 ss into first dc.

Cotton wool holder

First strip
Flower motifs
Make 12 motifs as motifs for Tissue Holder leaving 1 petal free between joinings and joining last motif to first motif to correspond.

Edgings
With right side facing, attach thread and work as edging for side of tissue holder for 8 rows. With right side facing, attach thread to opposite side of motifs and work as edging for side of tissue holder for 4 rows.
5th and 6th rows: As 7th and 8th rows of edging for side of tissue holder.
Work another strip in same manner, but do not fasten off.

Joining
As joining of tissue holder.

Roller holder

Base
Commence with 5 ch.
1st row: 15 dbl tr into 5th ch from hook, 1 ss into 5th of 5 ch.
2nd row: 4 ch, 1 dbl tr into same place as ss, * 3 dbl tr into next dbl tr, 2 dbl tr into next dbl tr; repeat from * ending with 3 dbl tr into next dbl tr, 1 ss into 4th of 4 ch.
3rd row: 4 ch, 1 dbl tr into same place as ss, * 1 dbl tr into next dbl tr, 2 dbl tr into next tr; repeat from * ending with 1 dbl tr into next dbl tr, 1 ss into 4th of 4 ch.
4th row: 4 ch, 1 dbl tr into same place as ss. * 1 dbl tr into each of next 2 dbl tr, 2 dbl tr into next dbl tr; repeat from * ending with 1 dbl tr into each of next 2 dbl tr, 1 ss into 4th of 4 ch.
Continue in this manner for 6 rows more, increasing 20 sts on each row and having 1 dbl tr more between each increase on each row.
11th row: As previous row increasing 10 sts.

12th row: As previous row increasing 14 sts. (224 sts.)
13th row: 1 dc into same place as ss, working into back loop only, work 1 dc into each dbl tr, 1 ss into first dc.
14th row: 4 ch, 1 dbl tr into each dc, 1 ss into 4th of 4 ch.
15th row: 4 ch, 1 dbl tr into each dbl tr, 1 ss into 4th of 4 ch. Fasten off.

Side
First strip (lower strip)
Flower motifs
Make 16 motifs as motifs for tissue holder, leaving 1 petal free between joinings and joining last motif to first motif to correspond.

Edgings
With right side facing, attach thread and work as edging for side of tissue holder for 8 rows.

Joining
As joining of tissue holder.
With right side facing, attach thread to opposite side and work as edging for side of tissue holder for 4 rows.
5th and 6th rows: As 7th and 8th rows of edging for side of tissue holder.

Second strip (middle)
Flower motifs
Make 16 motifs joining as before.

Edgings
With right side facing, attach thread and work as edging for side of tissue holder for 4 rows.
5th and 6th rows: As 7th and 8th rows of edging for side of tissue holder.

Joining
As joining of tissue holder.
With right side facing, attach thread to opposite side and work as first side for 6 rows. Fasten off.

Third strip
Flower motifs
Make 16 motifs joining as before.

Edgings
With right side facing, attach thread and

work as edging for side of tissue holder for 4 rows.

5th and 6th rows: As 7th and 8th rows of edging for side of tissue holder.

Joining

As joining of tissue holder.
With right side facing, attach thread to opposite side and work as edging for side of tissue holder for 7 rows.

Heading

1st row: 3 ch, 1 tr into each dc, 1 ss into 3rd of 3 ch.

2nd row: 4 ch, 1 dbl tr into each of next 4 tr, * 3 ch, miss 3 tr, 1 dbl tr into each of next 5 tr; repeat from * ending with 3 ch, 1 ss into 4th of 4 ch.

3rd row: 3 ch, 1 tr into each of next 4 dbl tr, * 3 tr into next sp, 1 tr into each of next 5 dbl tr; repeat from * ending with 3 tr into next sp, 1 ss into 3rd of 3 ch.

4th row: 1 dc into same place as ss, 1 dc into each of next 2 tr, * 3 ch, 1 dc into last dc, 1 dc into each of next 8 tr; repeat from * omitting 3 dc at end of last repeat. Fasten off.

Braid cord, *make 2*

Using double thread, commence with 2 ch, then holding this between the finger and thumb of the left hand, work 1 dc into the first ch made, turn, 1 dc into foundation loop of 2nd ch made, inserting hook into back of loop, * turn, insert hook into 4 loops at side, thread over and draw through 4 loops, thread over and draw through remaining 4 loops; repeat from * for 27 ins or length required. Fasten off. Damp and pin out to measurements.

To make up

⅝ in seam allowance has been given on all pieces.

Tissue holder

Cut 1 piece of fabric 10¼ × 16¾ ins and 1 piece 3 × 10 ins for facing.
Run line of basting stitches lengthwise on centre of fabric. With wrong sides together place facing centrally to main section covering line of basting stitches. Baste shape for opening 1 in wide × 8 ins long and machine stitch. Cut round opening leaving small seams and turn facing to wrong side. Fit cover over box, mark position of corner seams and machine stitch on wrong side. Trim seams and press open. Turn back hem along lower edge and machine stitch. Slip crochet over cover and secure.

Cotton wool holder

Cut 1 strip of fabric 9¼ × 14½ ins.
With right sides together machine stitch across short ends. Trim seam and press open. Turn back hems across top and lower edges and stitch. Slip crochet over fabric and secure. Insert container.

Roller holder

Cut 2 pieces 7¾ ins in diameter for base and 1 piece 10½ × 21¾ ins for side.
Cut 1 piece of cardboard 6½ ins for stiffening base.
With right sides together machine stitch across short ends of side piece.
Trim seam and press.
With right sides together stitch round base leaving an opening to insert stiffening.
Trim seam and turn to right side. Insert stiffening and slipstitch opening. Place side piece in position to base and stitch. Turn back hem across top edge and stitch. Insert to wrong side of crochet and secure.

Pincushion

Materials: Coats Mercer-Crochet no. 20
(20 grms).
1 ball.
This model is worked in shade 439 (Rose
Madder), but any other shade of Mercer-
Crochet may be used.
Milward steel crochet hook 1·25 (no. 3), or size
to fit tension (gauge).
¼ yd velvet, 36 ins wide.
Foam chips or kapok for stuffing.

Tension (gauge):
Size of motif – 4 ins diameter.

Measurements: Finished size of pin cushion
4½ ins diameter.

Wind thread 10 times round fore-finger and
slip strands off finger.
1st row: Into ring work 32 dc, 1 ss into first
dc.
2nd row: 5 ch, miss 1 dc, 1 tr into next dc, * 2
ch, miss 1 dc, 1 tr into next dc; repeat from *
ending with 2 ch, 1 ss into 3rd of 5 ch.
3rd row: 1 dc into same place as ss, * 10 ch,
1 dc into 2nd ch from hook, 1 hlf tr into next
ch, 1 tr into each of next 7 ch, 1 dc into next tr
on previous row (a spoke made); repeat from *
ending with 1 dc into base of first 10 ch made.
(16 spokes).
4th row: Ss to tip of first spoke, 1 dc into tip of
same spoke, * 7 ch, 1 dc into tip of next spoke;
repeat from * ending with 7 ch, 1 ss into first
dc.
5th row: 5 ch, 1 tr into same place as ss, * 3 ch,
1 dc into next sp, 3 ch, into next dc work 1 tr
2 ch and 1 tr (shell made); repeat from * ending
with 3 ch, 1 ss into 3rd of 5 ch.
6th row: 1 ss into sp, 5 ch, 1 tr into same sp,
* 4 ch, 1 dc into next dc, 4 ch, shell into sp of
next shell; repeat from * omitting shell at end

of last repeat, 1 ss into 3rd of 5 ch. Fasten off.
Damp and pin out to measurements.

To make up
Cut two circles of velvet 5½ ins diameter,
and one strip 28 × 2 ins for gusset. Join gusset
at narrow ends to form a ring and gather top
and lower edges. Draw up to fit circles and
tack in position, stitch ½ in from raw edges,
leaving an opening on lower circle, turn to
right side and stuff, sew opening neatly. Place
crochet centrally on top circle and sew in
position.